ON YOUR BIKE!

THE COMPLETE GUIDE TO CYCLING

WRITTEN BY MATT SEATON

Black Dog Publishing

Contents

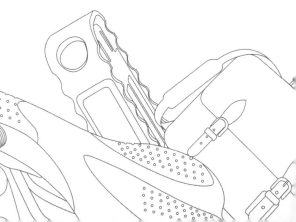

Evolutions and revolutions: the cultural history of the bicycle

Opposite: detail from Peugeot catalogue, 1934.

Below: detail from Raleigh catalogue, 1972.

The bicycle has played a unique part in human civilisation. It has travelled the world and, in its time, carried entire nations to work and sometimes even to war. Riding a bike has become a global experience, as universal as wearing a wristwatch or using a mobile phone. Its simplicity and utility have made it, in survey after survey, one of the most popular inventions in human history.

For what is a bicycle in its essentials? A plain lozenge-shaped frame fashioned out of metal tubing, two wheels made from wire spokes, a saddle, handlebars and cable-pull brakes, cranks, chain and cog—all designed to be light yet strong. Since its invention, we have discovered penicillin, split the atom and sent men to the moon, but that basic template of the bicycle has changed remarkably little for more than a century. The bicycle is a beautiful idea, so perfectly realised that it defies improvement.

But the bike is more than a machine; it is a friend. For everyone who has ever learned to ride one, the bicycle is always associated with a first taste of freedom and independence. The slogan of one of America's first great cycle manufacturers read "cycling is like flying" and, for many people who bought a Columbia bike at the turn of the nineteenth century, the raw excitement of travelling at speed under their own power would be the closest thing to the flight of birds they

would ever experience. And to each of us growing up the bicycle grants this epiphany. The thrill of travelling under one's own power, faster than walking, faster even than running, and for far less effort, never ceases to feel magical. The bicycle continues to do what it reliably always did— deliver the promise of personal transportation in a wonderfully cheap, practical and, above all, pleasurable form.

The Victorians bequeathed us many things of great value—from the idea of universal suffrage to the water closet—but was ever one loved more than the bicycle? And we have good reason to be grateful. From when we are five to 85 (and beyond), our friend the bicycle keeps us healthy by exercising our hearts and lungs without wearing out our joints and bones. In towns, the bicycle makes it possible for us to make trips of several miles, door to door, without undue exertion and in good time. In the country, we can travel long distances and admire the landscape even as

we smell the blossom on trees and observe the life in the hedgerow. And today, the bicycle has found a new role in the vanguard of environmental sustainability. Clean, green and socially useful—it ticks all the policy boxes. While motor manufacturers plough millions into technologies such as fuel cells in an effort to devise a true zero-emissions vehicle, many of us are still using the original and the best zero-emissions vehicle: the bicycle.

And that is the final wonder of the bicycle—that it has come round again—or that we have come back to it. For a time, in the second half of the twentieth century, people in the West seemed to fall out of love with the bicycle and forget its virtue. Instead of being the agent of modernity, it came to seem antiquated and quaint. By the 1960s cycling had become the second-class choice, the poor relation in road transport. Entire towns and cities were designed around the priorities of motorists, while cyclists were planned almost out of existence. It has taken several decades of a mounting crisis of cities choked by congestion and people choked by pollution for the realisation to set in that we were mistaken about the place of the bicycle in our future. Perhaps what we can see now is that the story of the bicycle has at its heart a powerfully redemptive theme. Its human scale, utility, environmental friendliness, and the sheer pleasure it has to offer its rider, all make the bike a winner once again.

Not that the car as the dominant mode of personal transport will disappear any time soon. For many people, most perhaps, the car will continue to be king. But the motor industry is having to evolve for a world where sustainability, safety and quality of life are taking over as priorities from our 'primitive' desires for power, speed and status. The energy used to manufacture a single car, it has been calculated, is sufficient to make a thousand bicycles. In the new era of environmental consciousness, the bicycle has energetically bounced back. Instead of being seen as a nuisance or joke, the bicycle has become part of the solution to the congestion that clogs the arteries of our cities.

Back in the 1960s, the novelist and philosopher Iris Murdoch wrote that "the bicycle is the most civilised form of transport known to man, while other forms grow daily more nightmarish"—an observation that has only become more resonant with the passage of time. Today we can begin to see that, far from being driven to extinction, the bike looks set to outlive the era of 'the great car economy'—or at least the era of the internal combustion engine economy. It is a safe prediction now (and it was not always so) that people will be riding bicycles long after the last car that ran on mineral oil has gone for scrap. It is almost as if the bicycle has managed to recycle the very idea of itself.

Automobiles are SO last year.

Wake up and smell the exhaust.

2005
Critical Mass

Early days

The bicycle's origins lie in the dreams of the pioneering engineers of the late eighteenth and early nineteenth centuries. They imagined a mechanical horse that would enable the individual to travel under his own power—without needing to stop for his animals to be fed and watered, let alone groomed and stabled.

One such visionary was Karl von Drais, a minor baron from Karlsruhe in Germany, who managed land for the Duchy of Baden. He failed in his first project, to devise a horseless carriage for several passengers. But in 1817, he devised a running machine for one person— the genetic antecedent of the bicycle. It essentially comprised a pair of wheels connected by a frame, with a hand-steerer at the front and a seat between the wheels that allowed the riders' feet to reach the ground in order to provide propulsion.

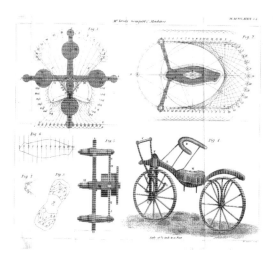

This early velocipede, or *Draisienne* as it was called, became quite a fad, and interest in the concept soon spread to France and England, where it became known as "the hobby horse", and even across the Atlantic, to the eastern seaboard of America. By 1819, there were riding schools in London and New York. This new craze met a mixed reception: the running machine enthusiasts were much mocked by satirists, and in New York, where the poor state of the roads meant that there was widespread use of the sidewalk, there was soon an outright ban on velocipeding in the city. Bad roads were a problem, but it was its lack of any transmission, other than the rider using his legs to run, that limited

Below: the Lefevre velocipede, which uses a power transmission system of pedals and levers to push the vehicle forward. In this way, the rider exerts a vertical force far more efficient than the horizontal or downward kicking forces of its predecessors.

the *Draisienne* and similar machines to a temporary phenomenon. The challenge to improve on the hobby horse design passed to the amateur mechanics and entrepreneurial engineers who flourished during the Industrial Revolution. By the 1840s, designers had begun to experiment with versions of a foot-treadle system that powered the rear wheel. Arguably, these were the first true bicycles, but they remained prototypes. The next major development in the velocipede was to add cranks and pedals to the front wheel, so that the rider no longer powered the machine by pushing off the ground and running, but by balancing entirely on the velocipede and pedalling.

By the mid 1860s, a Parisian craftsman named Michaux was producing such a machine at the rate of more than one a day from his workshop on the Champs Elysées–the avenue which today, appropriately enough, always stages the end of the Tour de France. By the end of that decade, the design was considerably improved by the addition of a solid rubber tyre, which made riding the *Michauline* a slightly less hair-raising

experience. But with their heavy, rigid frames and solid-spoked wheels that closely resembled those used for horse-drawn carriages, comfort was still in short supply. Not for nothing did this early type of bicycle become widely known in the English-speaking world as "the boneshaker".

Nevertheless, the pedal-powered velocipede was a major advance, and saw a revival of popular interest by the late 1860s: the schools reopened, the first races were run, and, perhaps most notably of all, the first female participants in the velocipeding phenomenon emerged. This new development was greeted by a combination of salacious interest and moral panic, which tended to focus on whether such an athletic activity was appropriate for women. A central theme was thus established for the coming decades: the bicycle became a major ally of women in their quest for greater freedom from restrictive social convention, but they had to battle for it. This meant fending off a conservative, yet often prurient moralism that expressed anxiety about the supposed danger of cycling to their reproductive health, and the indecency of the inevitable dishevelment of their dress. It was not easy to pedal, after all, without showing a bit of ankle.

The golden age

Below: the 1886 Boneshaker.

Below: the 1886 Boneshaker.

The problem with the bicycle as far as it had developed before the 1880s was that its speed was limited by the direct drive of its crank mechanism. One revolution of the pedals corresponded to one revolution of the wheel. It does not take a huge effort of imagination to see that the machine's terminal velocity would be limited by how fast its rider could pedal—and this speed would be reached rather soon. In 1869, an expatriate Englishman named James Moore won a velocipede race from Paris to Rouen, a distance of 123 kilometres. His average speed was 12kph (7.5mph), and he was using an outsize front wheel to achieve even that pace.

In fact, Moore was ahead of his time in setting the trend for bigger wheels. In the quest for speed from these front-wheel drive machines, front wheels became bigger and bigger—on the principle that if one pedal revolution must equal one wheel revolution, then you do well to make the distance covered by the wheel as large as possible. Hence the era of the high wheeler, or 'Penny Farthing' as it was nicknamed (thanks to the eccentric appearance of one large wheel at the front and one small one behind).

Improbably perhaps, since these large machines were not easy to mount and dismount and magnified the risk of injury by the height from which the rider would fall in an accident, the high wheeler became very popular. Numerous clubs and societies of riders formed, catering to the athletically-minded gentleman amateur. These clubs organised rallies and rides, and members would wear matching uniforms of fitted jackets with brass buttons and tight britches so that their cavalcade resembled

Above: Carl Paulson, an early high wheel enthusiast, in North Dakota, 1931.

Above right: a bicycle club in 1885.

something between a squadron of cavalry and a convention of postal messengers. One of the earliest such associations—one that survives to this day—was the Pickwick Bicycle Club, formed in 1870 (and named under the mistaken impression that Charles Dickens liked to ride a velocipede).

The high wheeler's ungainly looks tend to conceal the fact that they represented a substantial technological advance on the *Michauline*-type velocipede—especially in the science of wheel building. Rims, now of steel, where wood had commonly been used before, were being manufactured in hollow-section, providing the major benefit of strength combined with weight-saving. Bearings had improved, but above all the spoking system had changed entirely—from solid struts to wire. In effect, the hub was now suspended between the circumference of the rim, as in a modern bicycle wheel, where stresses are balanced between opposing spokes. The new wheels were strong and light, and while still rigid, contained a degree of compliance, which improved the bicycle's comfort and handling.

By the mid 1880s, the high wheelers had serious competition with the advent of the first 'Ordinaries', as these bicycles with equal-sized wheels were dubbed to distinguish them from their high and mighty cousins. What made the Ordinary possible was the development of rear-wheel drive by attaching a chain and sprocket mechanism to the cranks. This accomplished two very useful tasks at once: it enabled gearing and so eliminated the need for very large wheels. The chain drive transmission of the bicycle is both remarkably simple yet wonderfully effective: with a 98 per cent ratio of power out to power in, it is in fact one of the most efficient machines ever devised. The gearing that was possible meant that the rider was brought down from his eyrie-like perch and could now more than match the performance of the Penny Farthing—with only a fraction of the high wheeler's risk of an unscheduled dismount. For this reason, the new model bike became known as the 'Safety Bicycle'.

By 1888, in Britain, Safety Bicycles were outselling high wheelers by six to one. That was also the year in which a Scottish veterinarian living in Belfast named John Boyd Dunlop perfected something he had been working on for his son's tricycle: an air-filled inflatable tyre. The pneumatic tyre was a miraculous gift to the Safety Bicycle: it enhanced the rider's comfort immeasurably; it vastly improved road-holding and handling; and it made bicycles faster and more efficient. Dunlop's pneumatic made him a personal fortune, but it also meant that the bicycle—in a form that would be instantly recognisable today—had finally come of age. The story of the bicycle runs in many ways parallel to the history of the Industrial Revolution. It was mass production that made the bicycle, with its precision-engineered parts, possible.

Without the advances in technology and manufacture that accrued through the nineteenth century, the bicycle could never have evolved beyond a mere curiosity and toy of the leisured rich.

The bicycle and society

Below: an 1896 advertisement for a Primley bicycle. The price had already dropped substantially by this point, and was set to fall further.

By the early 1890s, factories were turning out bicycles in hundreds of thousands. What had been an artisanal enterprise a mere 20 years earlier was now a major industrial concern. Mass production brought the bicycle for the first time within reach of the lower orders. The high wheeler clubs had been almost exclusively the preserve of the gentry; now cycling was enjoyed by the lower middle class and aspirant working class. By the turn of the century, a bicycle in America could be bought for under $20–about the same as the price of a suit of clothes. "The two sections of the community which form the majority of 'wheelmen' are the great clerk class and the great shop assistant class", reported *The Cyclist* in 1892.

The socialist thinker and novelist HG Wells noticed the effect of the bicycle in transforming personal mobility into social mobility. In Wells's seminal cycling novel, *The Wheels of Chance*, published in 1896, the main protagonist is a draper's assistant, named Hoopdriver, who goes on a cycle tour. As literary fiction it may be negligible, but as a social document, it is fascinating. Hoopdriver's love interest, Jessie, is Wells's take on the 'New Woman'–the cultural antecedent of the Suffragettes who, a generation later, fought for women to have the vote. An independent young woman, Jessie is no longer confined by corsets and petticoats: she has taken to the road unchaperoned in a form of 'rational dress'. In the 1890s, the bicycle became a key battleground for the Rational Dress Society, which campaigned

vigorously for women to be freely permitted to wear practical, utilitarian clothing, including bloomers (a baggier version of the britches worn by men, originally attributed to an American lady, Amelia Bloomer). Hoopdriver finds himself astonished by the adaptations of Jessie's dress—she wears some kind of convertible skirt, a bifurcated garment that had become popular with female cyclists.

Because it gave freedom of movement to groups and classes of people who had had no such independence, the bicycle was synonymous with progress, opening up new opportunities and relaxing old social boundaries. In a very real sense, the first wave of female emancipees arrived on a bicycle. And such change was sometimes controversial. Bloomers, bicycles and the New Woman became so synonymous in the public mind that when, in 1897, Cambridge students demonstrated against women being allowed to take degrees at the University, they displayed an effigy of a woman in bloomers on a bicycle opposite the Senate House.

Feminism was not the only '-ism' to advance its cause through cycling. The 1890s was a great period in the growth of trade unionism and workers' associations. Here, too, cycling played a part. In Germany, the bicycle was pressed into the service of social democracy by the formation of the Workers' Cycling Federation, Solidarity—colloquially known as the 'red hussars of the class struggle' for their cycle-borne propaganda activities. On the eve of the First World War, the federation boasted 150,000 members.

The British equivalent, though on a smaller scale, was the Clarion Cycling Club, which had branches nationwide and its own distinctive subculture—a very English bohemianism, inspired in part by the socialist writing of Robert Blatchford, author of *Merrie England*. A few Clarion Clubs survive to this day, but with little hint of the heady atmosphere of its early incarnation, which grew out of the concept that the urban-dwelling, factory-working proletariat should have access to England's 'green and pleasant land'. There was more than a dose of romantic idealism in this movement—a William Morris-style pastoral dream that did not always connect with the reality of working-class life—but because it appealed to intellectuals, it had an influence out of proportion to the number of its adherents.

Celebrated playwright and author, George Bernard Shaw, was, like HG Wells, typical of the progressive intelligentsia of the time in his enthusiasm for cycling. Cycling was, he maintained, "a capital thing for a literary man". An energetic rider himself, he once bet a friend he could beat the train back to London from Dorking. Not only did he win the wager, the story goes, but he had time to reach each station on the way to greet his friend gloatingly on the platform. For Shaw and millions of like-minded souls, the bicycle was an integral part of a whole package of social progress: democracy, universal suffrage, women's rights, rational dress, recreation for the masses... nothing symbolised human dynamism so well. Cycling had become synonymous with progress.

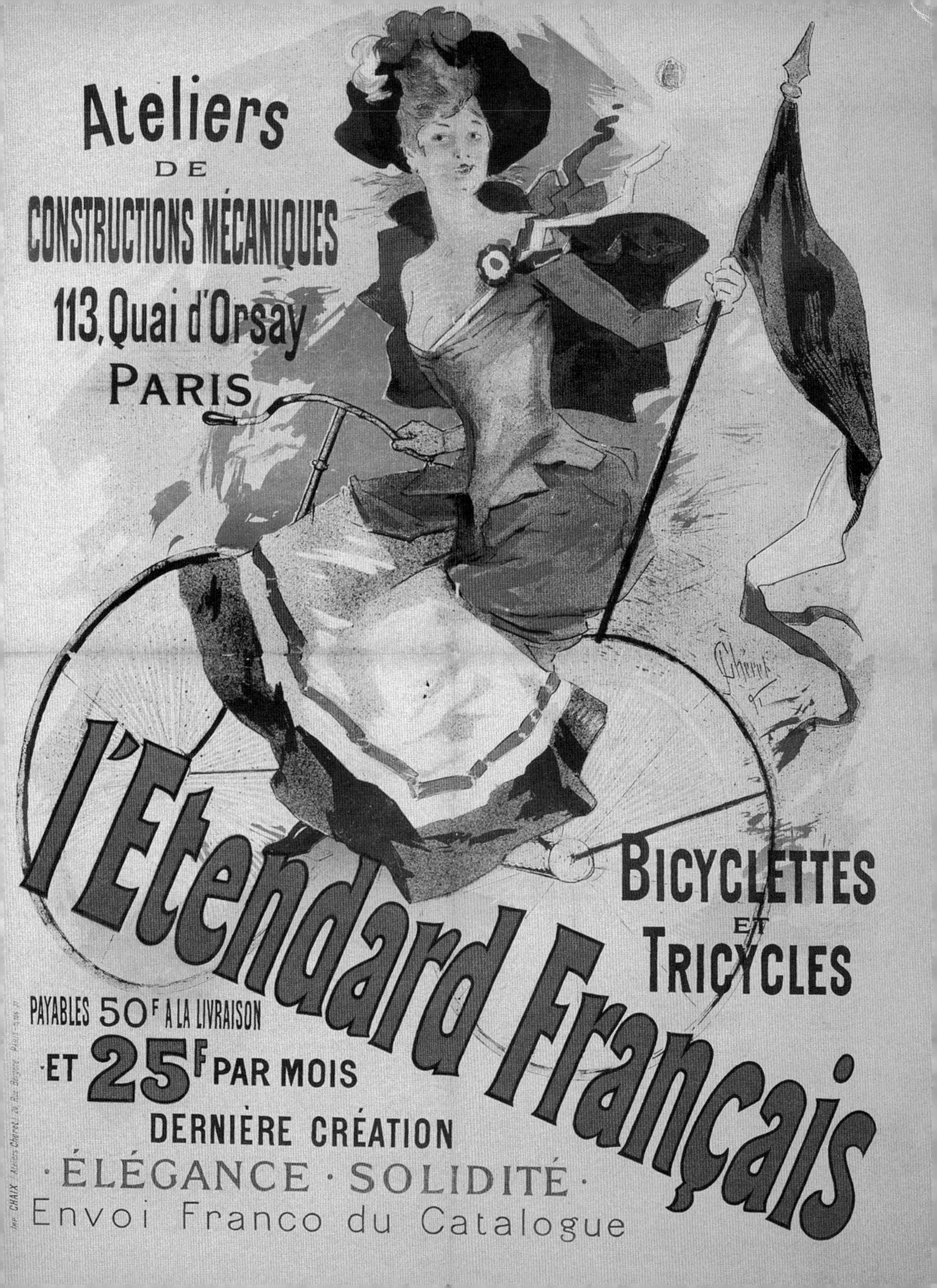
Ateliers
DE
CONSTRUCTIONS MÉCANIQUES
113, Quai d'Orsay
PARIS
l'Etendard Français
BICYCLETTES
ET
TRICYCLES
PAYABLES 50F A LA LIVRAISON
ET 25F PAR MOIS
DERNIÈRE CRÉATION
·ÉLÉGANCE · SOLIDITÉ·
Envoi Franco du Catalogue

The bike as icon

In his book, *One More Kilometre and We're in the Showers*, Tim Hilton, who is himself an art critic, notes that cycling has always attracted a disproportionate number of artists to its ranks. And he speculates, as one explanation among possible others, that cycling has an intrinsic aesthetic element. There is something pleasing, liberating, mind-expanding, and simply beautiful about the experience of cycling. Very true, and this may be in part why so many artists have also featured the bicycle in their work. It can be a gesture of affection, certainly, but it is also simply a measure of the extent to which cycling has entered people's lives and become part of everyday experience: in the most humdrum way, you might say, cycling means modernity.

And from modernity to Modernism—for the bicycle offered itself as emblematic of the new. It was not only the vehicle of the New Woman, but also, because of the almost Utopian harmony it proposed between man and machine, the model for a new spirit of mankind in the epoch of mass society and mechanisation. This optimistic early Modernist vision was largely shattered by the experience of the First World War, with its industrialised slaughter, but it is very visible in the work of the Italian futurists—notably, Umberto Boccioni, who explicitly celebrated the speed and power of the racing cyclist in his 1913 *Dynamism of a Cyclist*.

The sculptor Marcel Duchamp, most famous for scandalously entering a ceramic urinal for an exhibition, also incorporated bicycle parts into his sculpture. The philosophy of the Readymade was defined by André Breton as "manufactured objects promoted to the dignity of objects of art through the choice of the artist". In 1913 Duchamp took the front forks and wheel of a bicycle and screwed them upside down into a wooden stool, calling it an Assisted Readymade—since it had transformed a found object by displacing it from its familiar situation. The bicycle was barely 30 years old, but by Duchamp's day it had already become an everyday article so ubiquitous and utilitarian that this was as big a statement as putting a urinal on a plinth. 30 years later, Pablo Picasso practised a similar visual joke when he appropriated a bike saddle and curved handlebars from "a pile of jumble" to represent the head of a bull (*Tête de Taureau*). What both these artworks depended on was the surprise and pleasure on the part of the beholder at seeing the modest, friendly bicycle so wittily transformed.

Above: advertising poster for the
Monarch Cycling Co., 1894.

The French painter Fernand Léger frequently incorporated bicycles
into his canvasses. With their stylised figures intertwined with bikes,
and their brilliant colours, his paintings seem to express a renewed
optimism about the world that anticipated the exuberance of Pop Art.
And one of Pop Art's luminaries, Robert Rauschenberg, was another who
incorporated bicycles and bike parts into his pieces.

Two decades before Lance Armstrong's autobiography declared
that *It's Not About the Bike*, the German-American installation artist,
Joseph Beuys asked the question *Is it About a Bicycle?* In one of his last
major works, Beuys illustrated the events of his life in coloured chalk on a
sequence of blackboards, completing the piece by riding a bicycle whose
tyres left a trail of white paint across the blackboards—the cycle of life,
literally and metaphorically.

The appeal of the bicycle to artists is that it comes loaded both with
social symbolism and with personal emotional significance. It is a richly
associative object, conjuring up images, memories, feelings and hopes.
Few people feel neutral about bicycles. Almost all of us have, or have had,
some relationship with one—and I use the term 'relationship' advisedly,
since there are few things in our lives that we have such sentimental
investment in as our bike, whether it was the bike we learned to ride as
a child or the bike we use every day to go to work.

The bicycle might have got stuck as an icon of early Modernism,
celebrated mainly in the poster art of turn-of-the-century advertising,
but somehow, by keeping its place in our lives and our hearts, it has
always managed to renew symbolic value.

Decline and fall

Below: a Model T Ford, photographed by Robert Runyon.

The very success of the bicycle—especially its technological triumph—paved the way for its downfall. If the impulse behind the bicycle had been to invent a mechanical horse that could run on its rider's power, then the motor car came from the desire to build a carriage that did not need horses to draw it. The rudiments of the automobile were there with the bicycle—bearings, gears, chain-drive, pneumatic tyres—and all it took was the addition of the internal combustion engine. Hence the irony that so many car makers originally began as bicycle manufacturers—marques such as Peugeot, Humber, Sunbeam, Singer and Triumph.

In the United States Henry Ford's pre war revolution soon brought the automobile within the ambition of the working man. With the American economy powerfully resurgent after the Second World War—and without Europe's enormous burden of reconstruction—car ownership spread rapidly. Watch James Dean in *Rebel Without a Cause* today and that post war affluence is immediately apparent: it was 1958, but already American high school kids were driving their own cars. In the UK, food rationing continued into the 1950s, and a car was still very much a middle class luxury. Most Britons were still getting around by bike.

In the decade after the war, there were approximately 12 million regular cyclists in Britain—which meant that for rather more than one in five people, the bicycle was the main means of transport (and as a proportion of the adult working population, of course, 12 million would have been considerably higher than that). But as the 1950s gave way to the 60s and the fruits of the long post war boom finally arrived for ordinary people, the car acquired a status value that relegated the bicycle to being the poor man's mode of transport. The post war manufacturing economy was increasingly driven by car production—it was the single most expensive purchase most people were likely to make, but as such it was the one that most visibly displayed the prosperity people wished to show they had achieved. And the social and environmental costs of all these individual consumer choices were not yet apparent: the traffic congestion, the pollution, and the urban blight caused by car-centric town planning were still over the horizon during the post war boom.

If the entire economy was built on growth and expanding demand, how could you deny things to some that were granted to others? The dilemma was neatly encapsulated by the Labour politician, Anthony Crosland, writing in 1970. "My working class constituents... want cars, and the freedom they give on weekends and holidays. And they want package tour holidays to Majorca, even if this means more noise of night flights and eating fish and chips on previously secluded beaches. They [the affluent middle classes] want to kick the ladder down behind them."

Four years later, the total number of kilometres travelled by British cyclists hit an all-time low (four billion, down from over 20 billion in the early 1950s), and Britain's domestic bicycle manufacturing industry was in terminal decline. But if 1974 was the nadir of cycling's popularity and prestige, it was also the year of the OPEC oil crisis. Prompted in part by a hike in petrol prices, but in part also to a nascent environmental awareness and the beginning of the green movement, people took to their bikes again.

While the pattern of declining cycle use as transport was replicated across much of Europe in the second half of the twentieth century (with a few notable exceptions, such as The Netherlands), cycling itself did not lose prestige in the same catastrophic way that it did in Britain and America. And this was due in large part to the status of cycle sport in France, Italy, Spain and Belgium, especially. In Britain, with its busy roads and high population density, road racing always struggled to establish itself as an amateur sport. Indeed, at one period in the interwar years, it was outlawed altogether, as cyclists could be arrested by the police and charged with 'riding furiously'. This predicament led to a curious tradition still adhered to in time-trialling circles where races against the clock were held very early in the morning and on courses advertised only by code-numbers, so that their location would be known only to the racing fraternity. At the same time, Britain's cultural isolation from the rest of Europe made it virtually impossible for any professional racing team to

be viable on the domestic scene. In competition with football and other
national sports, British cycling was never able to attract the sponsorship
and publicity of its Continental cousin.

Cycle sport's lack of prestige in Britain is palpable–as you notice
when you cross the Channel. In many parts of Europe, motorists honk at
cyclists as a courtesy to let you know they are there, or sometimes even
for encouragement. In Britain, motorists honk at cyclists for one reason
only–because they think you are in their way and should get out of it.

Bike redux: the second industrial revolution

Below: pioneering new technology—the Cannondale Jacknife, a proposed design for a new type of folding bike by Phillippe Holthuizen.

The revival of cycling since the mid 1970s has many causes, but key to people's renewed interest has been the product itself. Today's bicycle would be instantly recognisable to the engineers of the bikes that our great-grandparents might have ridden. The basic structural concept at the heart of the bike has remained unaltered for over a century.

But, of course, there has been change. Enormous improvements in quality have come about, driven by the need of manufacturers for a competitive advantage—and finding one in innovation, quality and novelty. But the real innovation came from cyclists themselves—and specifically from 'bikies' in California, where two types of rider took their bikes off-road in search of new thrills. Both adapted and modified ordinary street bikes to race down challenging rough terrain. They eventually diverged and coalesced into two separate 'scenes'—BMX and mountain biking.

The BMX craze, which began in the 1970s, created a substantial new niche market for downsized bikes with a single gear and small wheels. Today, there are hundreds of BMX race tracks, and those who don't go in for the sprint races often prefer to hone their skills, performing tricks and stunts on ramps, much like skateboarders.

Mountain biking has been an even bigger phenomenon. It was pioneered by a first generation of inspired lunatics who got their adrenaline kicks riding down fire trails in Marin County, California, on 'clunkers'–heavy street cruiser bikes fitted with long handlebars and fat tyres. As the craze took off, some of these gonzo off-roaders–guys like Gary Fisher whose name became a brand in itself–turned entrepreneur to make bikes that would perform better. Two decades on, mountain biking has evolved into a mature sport, represented at the Olympics and with world championships. As importantly, mountain bikes have revolutionised the way bikes are designed, made and sold.

HETCHINS

The great mountain bike boom rescued the cycle trade from the doldrums in the 1980s with a fashionable new product. But while the first generation of bikes appealed to consumers with their chunky tyres and robust looks, they were desperately heavy for riding on roads—which, in the end, was how most of their buyers were going to use them most of the time. Selling more mountain bikes therefore became a quest to make better, lighter bikes. First, aluminium replaced steel as the frame-building material of choice, and then modern composites (carbon-fibre and resin compounds) came on the market. At the same time, componentry was heavily upgraded: bikes got more gears, with new and better shifting mechanisms; increasingly disc brakes replaced the previous rim-contact designs; front and rear suspension systems were borrowed from motocross and turned into lightweight kit suitable for bikes.

Those same Victorian craftsmen who built the Ordinaries of the 1890s would handle a modern bike with a mixture of respect, awe and envy. In recent years, the improved quality of manufacture and the constant refinement of design have produced better bikes for relatively lower prices year on year. Today's cycle consumer expects innumerable gears, flawless functioning, good looks, and all the latest extras such as hydraulic disc brakes. It was not so long ago that disc brakes were marketed as a desirable item on cars, let alone bikes.

But what the steady evolution of componentry in bicycles masks is that a revolution has taken place in the materials our bikes are made of. Once upon a time, all bikes were made of steel. Steel was excellent in many ways: cheap, tough, durable, and easy to cut and weld. At the top end of the market, bespoke frame builders used fine-gauge tubing to build remarkably light racing bikes. As recently as 1990, a bike that weighed under ten kilograms was a machine worthy of a professional racer. Nowadays, a full-suspension mountain bike will weigh in at less. In the quest for lightness, stiffness and strength, manufacturers have borrowed materials from the aerospace industry—aluminium, titanium and carbon-fibre—to develop frames that weigh less and perform better. And you no longer need to go to be measured for such a bike as if for a tailored suit or handmade dress; every high street bike shop will sell a range of such amazing machines.

The artisan craftsmen still survive, but they have had to adapt to the new world of miracle sub-seven kilogram bikes. Steel has actually made a modest come-back as a frame-building material, chiefly for connoisseurs and traditionalists who value its handling characteristics, but the modern mass market bike is made of aluminium alloy. Purists may say that aluminium has neither the longevity nor the 'feel' of a fine steel frame, but cheap bikes from chain stores never had much of that anyway: these were bikes made of no-nonsense, chunky cro-moly steel, compared with which an aluminium frame is streets ahead.

All of these technological developments have coincided with the globalisation of the industry. The shift of bicycle-manufacturing production to East Asia (first Japan, for Shimano components, and latterly to Taiwan, China, Korea and Vietnam for frame-making and assembly) has delivered better bikes at lower prices for Western consumers. It has also meant, though, the end of all large-scale domestic cycle manufacture in America and Europe. Apart from a few niche marques, virtually the whole market is supplied from the Far East. With a brand such as Raleigh, once Nottingham's biggest employer, only the design and marketing departments remain 'on-shore'. The manufacturing business has been exported to developing countries where labour costs are lower and environmental regulations laxer. This is the pattern of globalisation in every sector: someone somewhere is in effect paying for our cheaper, better goods with their lower wages, longer hours, fewer benefits and polluted environment.

From the budget to the boutique ends of the market, the modern bicycle is more advanced than ever. Yet its great charm is that it appears scarcely altered, wonderfully eternal in its mechanical simplicity—no one, for instance, has yet found a really good use for a microchip on a bike. But perhaps we should be looking forward to the day when the first 'fair trade' bicycle hits the high street.

The bicycle today

Opposite: a bicycle courier on the streets of New York. Photograph by Metin Alsanjak.

The revival of interest in cycling continues apace. In London, for instance, the number of cycle journeys has doubled in the past five years—an almost unheard-of case of a government target having to be revised upwards because it has been met ahead of time. The dogged efforts of cycle campaigners (such as the Cyclists Touring Club, Sustrans, and the London Cycling Campaign) are finally meeting with some success, and that is very encouraging. Their efforts are now very visible in cities throughout the UK: designated cycle lanes, the 'permissive' blue signage, advanced stop lines at traffic lights, and 'toucan' crossings on busy roads all attest to the fact that road traffic engineers and town planners increasingly see cyclists in a positive light—and no longer as a second-class citizen or plain nuisance.

More than that, though, these measures are also visible to motorists: when a driver sees a cycle lane marked on the road, he or she is getting a subtle, subliminal message that cyclists have a right to road space and priority. As other measures such as congestion charging, lower speed limits, and tighter enforcement of parking and lane discipline have gradually kicked in, the aggregate effect over time is to change the calculus for everyone's individual decisions about their choice of transport. In other words, there is now a slight 'push' away from cars, and a 'pull' towards cycling. That 'pull' was augmented by a further 'push' in 2005 after the terrorist attacks in London on 7 July left many people feeling anxious about travelling by public transport. More people got on bikes because they suddenly didn't want to be on buses or underground trains. Folding bikes, notably, did especially good business after 7/7.

The effect of more cyclists on the road creates a hugely beneficial positive feedback loop, or virtuous circle: because there are more cyclists, those who are cycling feel safer in cycling; the safer people feel cycling, the more they do it and the more those who try it occasionally stick to it permanently. And they find that the bikes themselves have improved since they cycled when they were kids. There is even excellent breathable waterproof rainwear, making year-round cycling more comfortable and practical.

Below: Critical Mass poster by Matt Bergstrom.

Opposite: Alistair Humphries spent over four years cycling around the world for charity. This photograph was taken during his time in Beijing.

With all this, cycling has begun to emerge from its hibernation, its long internal exile in the gulag of the tragically uncool. Cycling is once again coming to be seen as hip and desirable, useful and healthy. People can see that it is a very convenient way of getting their 30 minutes of daily exercise without having to force themselves to go to the gym after a day's work, and they can tell themselves that they are saving the planet at the same time. For the bicycle, there will, of course, be no return to the golden age of early Modernism, but it does suddenly seem more in tune with the zeitgeist than perhaps it has ever been since the 1890s.

Against this optimistic scenario of the bicycle resurgent, however, is the catastrophic decline of cycling in the newly industrialised world. In China, most glaringly, car ownership is becoming synonymous with social progress and the desire to display a long-awaited affluence. In Beijing, 1,000 new cars take to the streets every month—a transport and environmental crisis that took decades to produce in Western Europe is happening in the space of months, rather than years. The modest and subtle restraint of car use happening in some parts of the developed world should not obscure the fact that—despite the instability of the oil market and the evidence of global warming—much of the world is still in thrall to the great car economy. It seems as though many of the great cities of the developing world will have to go through the painful cycle of exponential traffic growth, marginalisation of cyclists and pedestrians, congestion, and urban blight, as politicians and policy makers reel before the unstoppable tide of the new car-owning classes.

Perhaps this is the great twenty-first century challenge for cycling campaigners: to export the knowledge of our own worst mistakes before others make them too.

We view ourselves not as the owners of bikes but as the caretakers.

Stephen Carter/USA

Opposite above: Stephen and his wife on their 1889 Columbia Tandem Tricycle for adults.

Opposite below: Stephen with his favourite bike, the Columbia Light Roadster.

1,000 people in a park wearing nineteenth century clothing and accompanied by hundreds upon hundreds of Penny Farthings, Ordinaries and velociepedes. It can only be one thing. The annual national meet of the Wheelmen.

The Wheelmen is a non-profit organisation dedicated to the preservation of the first 100 years of American bicycle heritage. There are around 1,300 members worldwide (most based in the United States and Canada) all of whom are committed to researching, riding and often restoring early bicycles, with many of them building collections that rival the best of museums. Based on bicycle clubs of the 1890s, the club is par-military in organisation and is run by an elected Commander, and beneath him a series of State Captains. The Commander for the year 2006 was Stephen Carter.

"We view the years 1816–1916 as the golden age of cycling and ourselves not as the owners of bikes and memorabilia but as the caretakers.... I am the caretaker of 30 bicycles and tricycles built prior to 1916 and another 20 built from 1920 through today... the centrepiece is an 1889 Columbia Tandem Tricycle for adults, while my favourite ride is a 53 inch Columbia Light Roadster built in 1891."

The Wheelmen recreate bicycle events of the early days, participating in parades, races, high teas and gala banquets in full regalia appropriate to the year of the bicycle they bring to the event. They aim to make the bikes as visible as possible to the public. Occasionally a larger expedition is embarked on—like the century ride of 100 miles on the antique bicycles. Stephen Carter took this one step further and actually rode his Columbia across America, following as close a route as possible to that of Thomas Stephens the cyclist, who in 1884 was the first person to make the trans-America journey on a bicycle.

"There are times I would love to go back to the days of the High Wheeler. To live in the time when the bicycle was evolving from iron frame with wagon wheels to lighter steel frame with a large front wheel and finally chain driven safety bikes. I personally enjoy dressing and acting as if in the age of the High Wheel.... Life was hard for the people of the 1890s, yet it was simpler as well. When I ride the High Wheel to one of our National Meets I can't help but think what a peaceful ride it would have been 100 years ago. I truly believe I could give up computers, cell phones, television and even radio. Maybe I was just born 140 years too late."

Your bike—and how to love it

Your choice of bicycle needs to be governed by the type of riding you
will be doing. A gorgeous racing bike will give you pleasure every time
you ride it, but if your only cycling is a daily commute through traffic,
you might want something less precious and more robust. That sort of
year-round use is remorselessly hard on components, and it's almost
impossible to preserve a beautiful paint job when you're constantly
locking and unlocking, and leaning your bike against railings and
street furniture. Then again, if most of your riding is recreational, you
hardly want to be lumbered with a sturdy workhorse for your weekend
excursions. You want a bike that really wants to take flight and roll for
miles. You need a bike that will feel like a dancing partner, rather than
a wrestling match. And if your thing is riding along canal paths and
country bridleways, and maybe some more adventurous off-road routes,
then you will need something with knobbly tyres, powerful brakes and
suspension, probably front and rear. A decent-spec mountain bike, in
other words.

But bear in mind that it's not a once-and-for-all decision. The more
you want to ride, the more likely it is that there will be occasions when the
bike you're riding seems less well adapted to the purpose than something
someone else has. People trade in bikes and change them all the time. You
can upgrade, either bit by bit, or all at once.

Buying a bike

The first rule is to figure out what type of bike you need and what type of bike you want. These may not be the same thing. How you solve that potential conundrum is a matter of budget and personal conscience. Be honest with yourself, and if you are going to err, then my advice would be to err on the romantic side: go for the bike you most desire, the one that you will really want to ride. Remember that there is a huge gulf between the figures for cycle ownership and the number of people who regularly ride: too many bikes bought sadly end up collecting dust in sheds and hallways. That is a powerful argument against what may seem the 'sensible' choice.

Spend, spend, spend...

The second rule is to spend to the hilt of your budget. You can buy a very reasonable bike for £300 ($500); for £500 ($900), you can buy a really good bike; for £800-£1,000 ($1,400-$1,800), you can buy something amazing. Above £1,000 the returns are diminishing, but £2,000-£3,000 ($3,500-$5,000) would get you a bike whose performance would be only infinitesimally inferior to the sort of machine Lance Armstrong would be riding. The point of buying as high as you dare is that the better the bike, the greater the pleasure it will bring you. The greater the joy, the more you will want to use it. The choice may seem bewildering and the distinctions between one bike and another either obscure or academic, but remember that the bike trade is a highly competitive environment. Under £1,000, certainly, price alone is a pretty reliable indicator of quality. You may feel that one bike is much like another if you go for a test-ride, but I guarantee that within a few months, you would be able to detect the difference that, for example, a better pair of wheels would make to your ride.

But save some for the rest

So buy the best bike you can, but remember that you are also likely to need to buy some accessories. Mudguards, lights, lock, helmet, and any number of additional extras can easily add £100-£200 ($170-$350) to your spend.

Getting fitted up

Before you part with any money, try to have a test-ride. Locate a shop where you find the staff helpful and informative (this may not be the case in the first store you enter). Not only should you be offered useful advice about the type of bike you want, but a careful fitting process should take place. In some shops, especially if you are buying an expensive road bike, this may involve quite a lengthy consultation with many measurements taken. If you are making a big purchase, allow time for this: it is essential you should be correctly measured and fitted. A frame can be the wrong size by as little as ten millimetres—and really be wrong for you.

The two basic measurements are reach and height. That is, the distance from the saddle to the handlebars, and the distance from the saddle to the pedals. Positions vary from bicycle type to type: a road bike, designed for speed and aerodynamic efficiency, will typically demand a more low-profile, stretched-out position than a commuting hybrid, built for comfort and the better all-round vision of a more upright position. Both height and reach are adjustable on any given bike, but within relatively small tolerances. It is important to match your physique and your needs to the correct size of bike, and you should feel that you have had comprehensive and expert advice from a shop before you make any purchase.

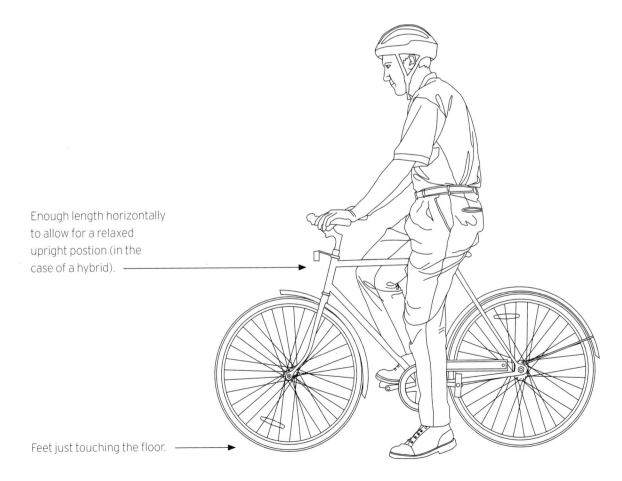

Enough length horizontally to allow for a relaxed upright postion (in the case of a hybrid).

Feet just touching the floor.

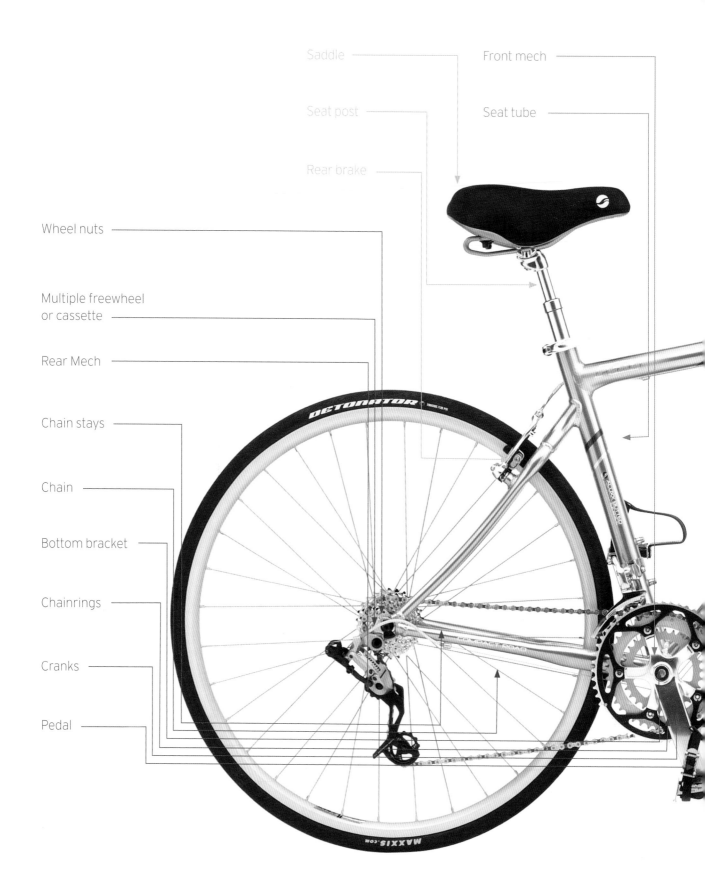

Saddle

Front mech

Seat post

Seat tube

Rear brake

Wheel nuts

Multiple freewheel
or cassette

Rear Mech

Chain stays

Chain

Bottom bracket

Chainrings

Cranks

Pedal

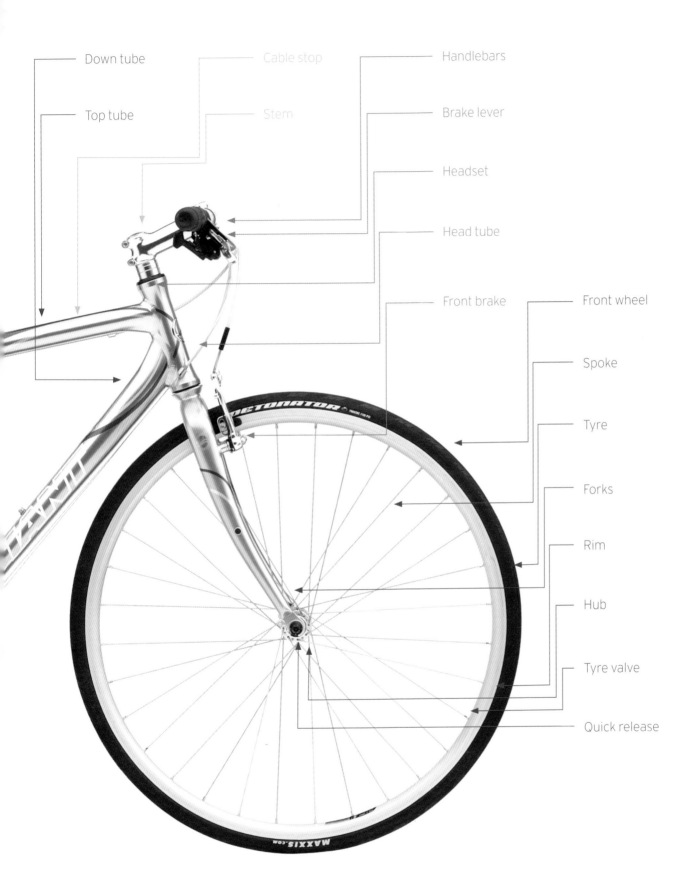

Down tube

Top tube

Cable stop

Stem

Handlebars

Brake lever

Headset

Head tube

Front brake

Front wheel

Spoke

Tyre

Forks

Rim

Hub

Tyre valve

Quick release

Types of bicycle

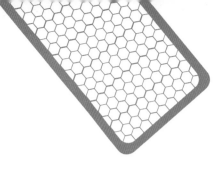

The road bike

Below: the Cannondale Six13 road bike made with a combination of aluminium and carbon tubing is one of the lightest of its kind.

Also known as the racing bike, this looks essentially like what the riders in the Tour de France use. The main distinguishing feature is the distinctive 'drop' handlebars, which give a variety of possible hand positions but favouring a low, racing-style position on the bike. The saddle is set slightly higher than the bars, emphasising the rider's low-profile stance. In all modern road bikes, the brakes and gear shifters are integrated, forming a single unit operated by each hand. The chief component brands in this market are Shimano and Campagnolo. Both are excellent in quality, have slightly different operations, and have their own loyalists among users.

The frame game

The frame may be made of aluminium, especially at the lower end of the price range. Steel is also still used, but tends now to be a niche market frame material. Carbon-fibre—light, stiff and strong—is increasingly becoming the frame manufacture of choice, and carbon frames are becoming cheaper year on year. Titanium is another popular choice, but because it is relatively difficult and expensive to work, and so tends to be a high-end option.

Each frame material has slightly different 'ride' and performance characteristics. Aluminium, the most affordable, has the reputation of being very light and stiff, but rather harsh in comfort terms, but many frame designs are now engineered to take account of this, and you should make your own judgment based on a test ride. Aluminium is also said to fatigue and lose its best properties over time; but, realistically, this is only likely to occur within the lifetime of most frames by very demanding use (such as being ridden hard and often by a heavy and powerful racer).

Compact' geometry' frames are now very widespread. These are frames where the top tube, horizontal in traditional bike frames, slopes downwards towards the back–in imitation of the smaller, 'tighter' mountain bike frames. There may be some advantage of stiffness and weight saving in compacts, but the difference is marginal (if even measurable). In many cases, frames can be supplied either with sloping or horizontal top tubes, and it really comes down to an aesthetic preference on your part.

Wheel deal

Wheels are sized as '700c' (that is, 700 millimetres in diameter). Rims are aluminium alloy or, if you go very up-market, carbon. Spoke patterns vary considerably, from traditional laced arrangements to flat 'aero' spokes in asymmetric patterns or radially arranged. Lightness and rigidity are considered virtues, but strength and durability matter too. Most wheels sold to the public are designed to carry 'clincher' tyres, although the old-fashioned racing type of tubular tyre ('tub') is still favoured for some racing specialisms.

Most road bikes are sold without mudguards as standard. If you plan to use your road bike for long excursions only when the weather forecast is good, then it is reasonable to dispense with them. Purists feel that the classic lines and purposeful look of a racing bike are spoiled by adding mudguards. But unless you plan to race, in which case mudguards do add a weight and aerodynamic penalty, then they are highly advisable. Even a short, sharp rain shower can leave you with sodden feet and a wet bum. Mudguards also help protect your bike, particularly its crucial transmission parts, from the worst of the water, grit and grime.

All the gear

It is increasingly common for road bikes to be supplied with ten-speed cassettes–the common term for the cluster of sprockets on the rear wheel. Typically, these sprockets will have from 11 up to 25 or more teeth, giving a good spread of gear ratios. Classically, the rear sprockets are combined with two chainrings at the front. Front and rear derailleurs controlled by gear levers, left and right on the handlebars, move the chain from each chainring and up and down the sprockets respectively. Two chainrings at front with ten sprockets at rear therefore give 20 possible gears. In practice, the chain line from front to rear needs to be reasonably straight to be efficient and thus makes certain combinations of chainring and sprocket less efficient, so that you would only ever use 17 or 18 of the theoretical 20 gear ratios.

In recent years, chainsets with triple chainrings at the front have become popular for road bikes not intended for pure race use–one of many examples of technology transfer from mountain bikes. However, the triple has also been joined by the 'compact' chainset–this has a conventional double chainring, but with smaller ratios–aimed at the non-racing but serious recreational cyclist. Where a racing bike would typically have chainrings with 53 and 39 teeth, a compact might have rings of 50 and 34. This is a very sensible measure since a ratio such as 53 by 12 will be used only by racing cyclists travelling at over 45 kilometres per hour and then only for a minority of the time. The compact chainset preserves the aesthetics of the pure racing bike, but with more sensible and realistic gearing for most users.

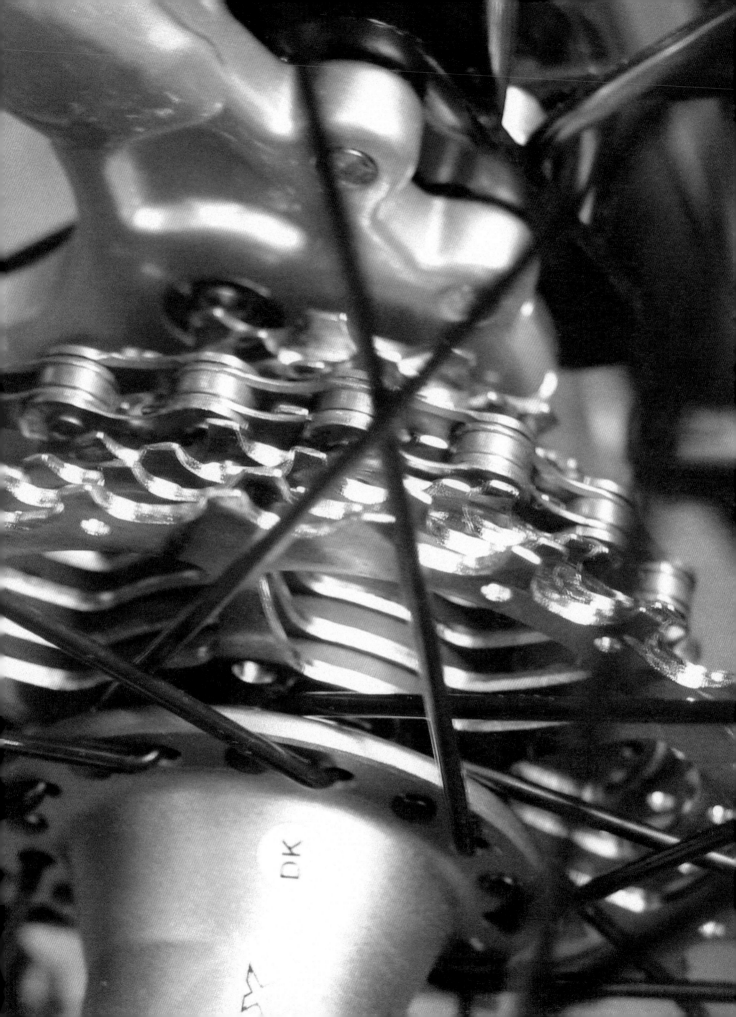

The mountain bike

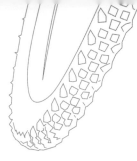

The mountain bike has been the locus of more technical development in recent years than any other type of bike. First, mountain bikes had more gears than any other bike before them, to cope with going up extreme gradients. And to make changing gears easier and faster, new designs of shifter appeared. Then these bikes evolved better, more powerful brakes to deal with going down extreme gradients. To the conventional 'diamond' frame of the bicycle was added, first, front suspension and, then, rear. Most mountain bikes now are of full-suspension design. Wheel and tyre design also had to adapt to a market where innovation and performance are generally valued ahead of straight cost.

Willing suspension

The result of all these developments are bikes that often look somewhat outlandish to traditionalists, but which are astonishingly effective for serious off-road riding on the kind of terrain that until recently would have defied being ridden on a bike at all. Many of the design features of modern mountain bikes—such as full suspension and hydraulic-operation disc brakes—have been borrowed inventively from moto-cross, but re-engineered to make the weight-savings necessary for a machine powered by nothing other than its rider's strength and endurance.

The first mountain bikes were very heavy and cumbersome by comparison. But they had the tremendous advantage of novelty and fashion on their side. Many were bought for their rugged, rough-tough looks alone—even though the over-engineered frames and knobbly tyres made them seriously inefficient for urban transport. Today's mountain bikes are much more sophisticated pieces of kit, and as the market has matured, they tend to be bought more for the original purpose they were intended for—off-road riding.

All downhill

In the arena of competition, mountain biking has bifurcated into cross-country and downhill racing. Downhill bikes are even more like moto-cross bikes without engines: their front forks are raked at a flatter angle for greater stability and the suspension will have greater travel. Racers can hit speeds of 80 kilometres per hour on off-road courses. Not surprisingly, a whole array of body armour, again much like that used by moto-cross riders, has been adopted to protect them from injury in the case of the inevitable 'offs'.

Clockwise from top: Marin Alpine Trail;
Cannondale Rush Team; Specialized P2;
Giant Reign 2; Marin Quake; Marin Rift
Zone.

For downhill racing bikes, strength is a more important consideration than weight, but for cross-country mountain bikes, where competitiveness depends on speed in climbing as well as descending, weight remains a major factor. Cross-country mountain bikes still have full suspension to aid fast descents, but have more conventional geometry and less travel in their suspension. There is also a play-off of mechanical efficiency against effective suspension–suspension tends to absorb some of a rider's energy so that a proportion of the pedalling force gets absorbed by the bike's 'bounce', rather than going directly down on the trail through the transmission. On the other hand, suspension can serve to optimise traction. Top-of-the-range mountain bikes have adjustable suspension so that they can be 'tuned' to suit particular courses or conditions–for instance, hard, rocky trails or soft, muddy ones. All this technology does not come cheap: a top-end mountain bike will tend to outprice a road bike of comparable quality.

Hybrids

Overleaf: an off-road cyclist rides the Specialized Epic Marathon.

Below: Giant FCR 4 Hybrid.

Hybrids have developed as a response to the consumer demand for a specifically urban bike. The popularity of mountain bikes adapted for use by commuting cyclists—swapping knobbly off-road tyres for faster-running slicks—made manufacturers realise that there was a new market for a new type of bike, something intermediate between a road bike and a mountain bike (or, more precisely, with the best features of both). A road bike, for example, is designed to make the rider stretch out in an aerodynamic position, whereas a mountain bike allows a more upright position, better for sighting and manoeuvring—a definite plus when cycling in busy city traffic.

Likewise, hybrids took the gearing and braking systems of mountain bikes but generally combined them with road bike-style rigid frames without suspension (superfluous for riding on flat Tarmac surfaces). Considerable variety remains. Some hybrids look more like urban mountain bikes, with compact frames and 26 inch wheels; others use the larger 700c wheels of road bikes and more open diamond frames. The common features tend to be triple chainsets and straight handlebars (rather than the 'drop' handlebars of road bikes), but some hybrids offer modern versions of hub gear systems.

Transport hub

In the hub gear, there is no external cassette cluster of sprockets; instead, the gears are contained within an enlarged rear wheel hub and are controlled by a cable mechanism. The advantage of hub gears is that they are more or less maintenance-free and, unlike derailleur systems, are hidden from the elements and road grime. Any marginal loss of performance with the hub gear is quickly compensated for by the fact that dirty, grease-clogged derailleurs soon lose their mechanical efficiency. If most of your riding is on city streets, then the hub gear is well worth considering. The five or seven gears they usually offer are more than adequate to the purpose; in fact, most of the gear ratios offered by triple chainsets of derailleur systems are superfluous.

Track bikes

I still feel that variable gears are only for people over forty-five. Isn't it better to triumph by the strength of your muscles than by the artifice of a derailleur? We are getting soft.... As for me, give me a fixed gear!

Henri Desgrange, *L'Équipe* article of 1902

There are two surprising features of the track bike. It has no brakes, and it has only one gear—both of which seem counter-intuitive. But the track bike is perfectly at home in the velodrome—the banked racing circuits, sometimes indoor and covered, sometimes outdoor and open to the elements.

Getting a fix

The track bike frame is much like a road bike's, and has similar drop handlebars. But unlike a road bike, the 'dropouts' in which the rear axle sits do not face downwards but backwards. And with a track bike, there is simply one chainset joined by the chain to a single rear sprocket. This rear sprocket is also fixed to the rear hub. In other words, there is no freewheel mechanism. The gear is thus 'fixed', which means that as long as the bike is in motion, the pedals must turn in a set ratio to the rear wheel. This takes some getting used to as a rider: while the bike is rolling, you cannot stop pedalling—try and you will get a shock, as the momentum of the bike forces the pedals round. There is no freewheeling on a track bike.

Below: the track bike is perfectly at home in the velodrome. Photograph by Vaughn Trevisanut.

Perpetual motion

Once mastered, this is actually quite a pleasant feeling. The effect of riding a single gear ratio means that the rider has to adapt his pedalling to the bike's speed; often this means pedalling rather faster—or at a higher cadence—than customary. Traditionally, this exercise has been held to improve pedalling style and efficiency. It is not dissimilar to the high-revving, 'spinning' style favoured by Lance Armstrong, for instance. In the past, using a fixed gear bike was said by coaches to improve a rider's *souplesse*—a French term best translated, perhaps, as fluency or fluidity.

The trend continues to this day, in that many racers incorporate riding a fixed into their winter training. This will usually be a track bike, adapted for the road by the important addition of at least a front brake, but often brakes front and rear. Brakes are not used on the track itself because riders are always travelling in the same direction and at more or less the same speed. Because everyone is riding a fixed gear, changes of speed by individual riders are relatively predictable and it is assumed that large groups of riders on a velodrome are safer if none of them has the ability to slow down suddenly by braking.

Courier chic

Although it takes some additional skills to ride a fixed gear bike, they are becoming increasingly popular as urban road bikes—at least, in cities where there are no long, steep hills. Cycle couriers often favour 'fixeds'. They are light, cheap, hassle-free to maintain and reliable. Being specialist items, they are also somewhat less attractive to thieves. Occasionally, you may see a bike messenger riding a pure track bike without brakes. It is possible to slow down and stop quite quickly on a track bike using leg strength alone to 'lock up' the back wheel, but it is a difficult skill; and riding a track bike without brakes on the road is definitely not recommended.

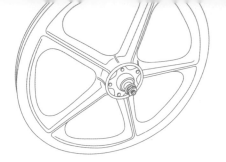

BMX bikes

Below: the Specialized Fuse BMX.

Opposite: BMX champion Tom Lynch's 'backyard jam'.

Like mountain biking, BMX biking was another trend that began in California in the late 1970s and early 80s. The BMX bike has even smaller wheels than a mountain bike, and a single-speed gear (that is, one chainring and one sprocket, rather like a track bike, but with a freewheel mechanism). BMX racing is fast and furious—essentially a sprint around a tight, oval-shaped circuit with severe undulations that have to be jumped. It is an extreme test of athleticism, handling skills and nerve. Although very much a subcultural scene, like skateboarding, BMX has produced some notable racing stars who have gone on to perform at the elite level in other cycling disciplines—such as mountain biking or track cycling.

BMX has brought whole generations of young people, who might otherwise have bypassed bikes altogether, into cycling by developing its distinct brand of hip urban identity. Just as popular as BMX racing is stunt-riding on BMX bikes with axle extensions that enable other foot positions than on the pedals. Riders in competition perform astonishingly acrobatic freestyle tricks on a series of ramps. The skills are similar and the competition as intense as in snowboarding or skateboarding.

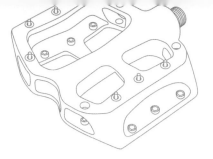

Cyclo-cross bikes

Below: the Cannondale Cyclo-cross Disc, known as such for its disc brakes, which allow for all-weather performance.

Cyclo-cross bikes—or plain 'cross bikes' to aficionados—are much like road bikes, but with a couple of adaptations for off-road racing. Cyclo-cross is a winter sport, particularly popular in Belgium, but with adherents in most north European countries and the USA. It involves racing around a circuit that is mainly off-road, sometimes with obstacles such as steps or hurdles that force a rider to dismount and carry his bike. These circuits can be ridden on a mountain bike, but they tend to be less technical and faster than a cross-country mountain bike course and so better suited to what is essentially a racing bike.

The chief differences between a cross bike and a road bike are that the cross bike is designed with much greater clearance around the wheels, so that accumulations of mud do not interfere with the rotation of the wheels. For this reason, they also have cantilever brakes. Finally, the 700c wheels are shod with knobbly tyres—closer in design to mountain bike tyres—to give greater grip on soft, slippery surfaces. Cyclo-cross races generally last approximately an hour for adults, less for juniors and youth riders. It is a sport that demands a high level of fitness, but also good handling skills and judgment. Many road racers use it as a way of maintaining fitness and having some competitive fun in the winter months.

Folding bikes

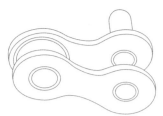

There has been a substantial niche market for folding bikes for several decades. The ever-popular design of Alex Moulton, the folding Brompton, has been in production since the 1960s. More recently, several manufacturers have taken up the challenge of producing a bike that can be quickly and easily folded and stowed. Rising petrol prices and parking charges, together with the utility of being able to carry a bike easily on public transport, have led to a resurgence of interest in folding bikes.

In order to collapse into a sufficiently small unit to be useful, folding bikes always have to 'break' the frame at some point with a hinge. Inevitably, this somewhat compromises the stiffness and rigidity of the frame, as well as adding to its weight. Folding bikes, therefore, are made for practicality, rather than performance. Their small wheels are also not always ideal for negotiating ill maintained urban roads. But the designs are highly ingenious, and for those who, for instance, want to combine a rush hour train journey with a bike ride, they are an effective and convenient transport solution.

Essential accessories

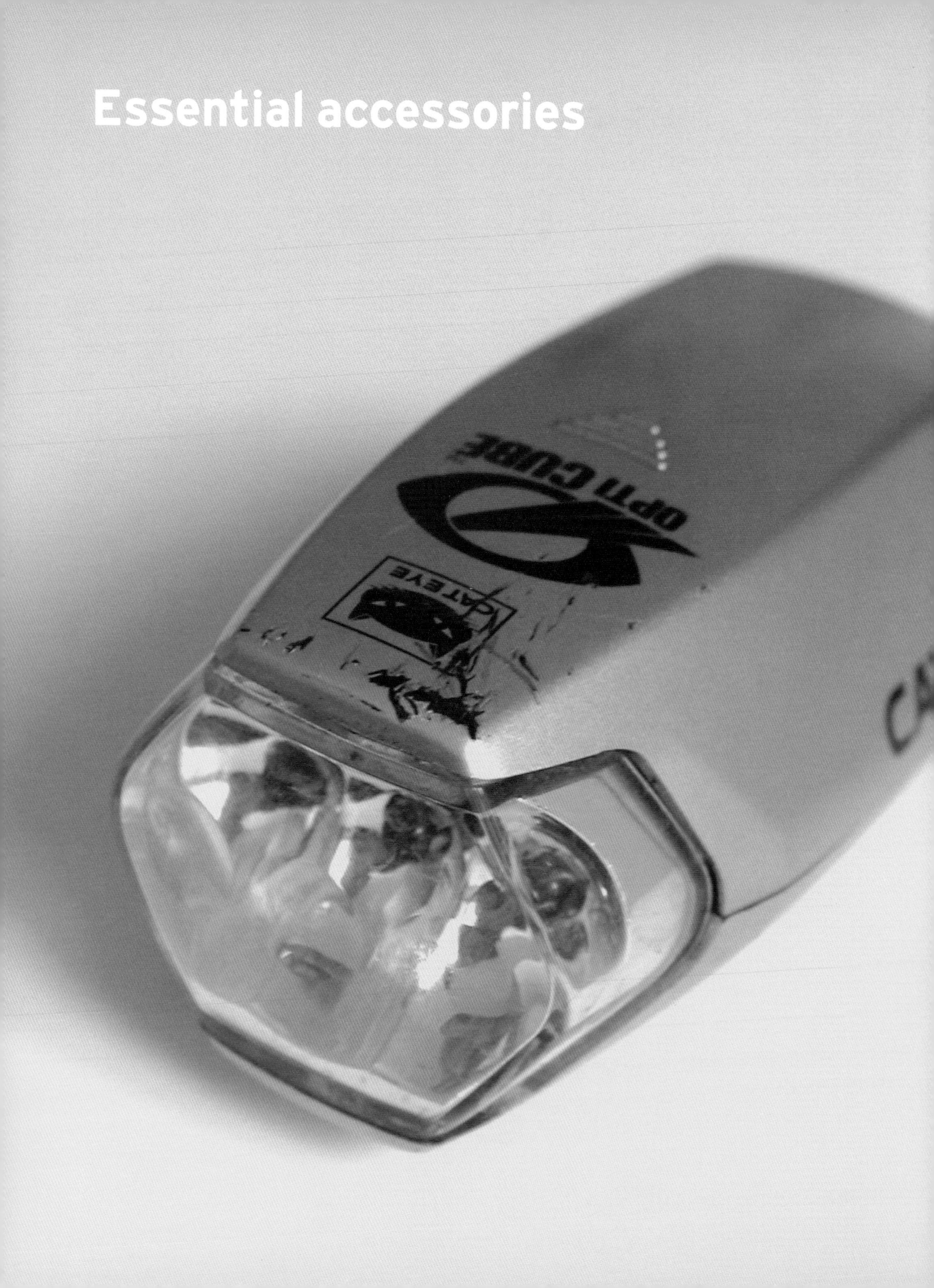

Security

Bikes do become friends, which is why theft is so hurtful. And avoiding losing an old friend is a very good reason to invest in a good lock. Obviously, if you are simply in the market for a racing bike that will never be left outside unattended, then a lock may be superfluous. But for any 'utility' or everyday bicycle, the lock will probably be your most important purchase after the bike.

Lock, stock and barrel

The bad news is that there is no lock that is completely, 100 per cent thief-proof. There are techniques for breaking virtually every lock: a simple hacksaw or medium-sized pair of bolt cutters will swiftly dispatch some. U-locks can be broken with a car-jack, or even a piece of scaffolding pipe. Even the toughest padlock and shackle can be attacked with an angle-grinder or by a freeze-and-shatter method of liquid nitrogen and a lump hammer. The old design of U-lock barrel could have its lock simply picked using the open end of a Bic biro!

What deters thieves is the length of time a lock will force them to work at breaking it in a public place. A lock able to resist assault for minutes rather than seconds will therefore do the trick in most circumstances. Unfortunately, lock strength and weight are closely correlated. A nice light cable lock is convenient to carry but will not save your bike from a thief with bolt-cutters. You need a good-quality U-lock, or a hardened-steel chain and padlock type. In practice, you should be spending at least £30 ($50) on a lock–or up to ten per cent of the value of your bike. Again, this is an area where a good bike shop should be able to offer useful, up-to-date advice.

A selection of U-locks, cable locks, chain locks and cuff locks by leading brands.

Immovable objects

Just as important as having a good lock, is knowing how to lock your bike up safely. There are a few straightforward rules to follow:

1. Your lock shackle should pass through either the front or the rear triangle of the frame, preferably through a wheel at the same time.

2. Ensure that you are locking your bike securely to an immovable piece of street furniture. Remember here that it is no good having a hardened steel chain and impregnable padlock if a thief can make short work of what you're locking your bike to with a simple hacksaw.

3. Try and leave as little slack as possible between the lock, your bike, and the object it is locked to. Anything that makes it harder for a thief to get to work with tools is worth doing. Avoid, for example, a situation where your padlock could be pulled down to the pavement—this deprives a thief of using the paving as an anvil for his hammer.

4. Try to lock your bike in a well-lit public area, preferably one that is likely to be covered by CCTV.

5. If your bike is new, consider removing decals or covering them with gaffer's tape. The less there is on your bike that identifies it as brand new, the safer it is likely to be. This is the only good argument for never cleaning your bike.

6. If you have quick-release wheels (these are the type that can be easily removed by pulling out the lever on the left-hand end of the axle), it is a good idea to ensure that both wheels are locked when leaving the bike in a public place. This can be achieved by combining a cable loop with your main lock. Another measure is to replace quick-release levers with a type that is tightened by an allen key. This is still more convenient to you than having nuts that need a spanner to tighten or loosen, but sufficient deterrent to the casual thief. Often on mountain bikes and some hybrids, the collar that secures the seatpost is also of quick-release type; it is best to replace this with an allen-key operated clamp (or resign yourself to removing and carrying with you the saddle and seatpost whenever you lock up—otherwise it will go).

7. Do register your bike with the police when you buy it. This is now swift and easy online and means that you do at least somewhat improve your chances of recovery should your pride and joy get pinched.

8. Finally, do consider insuring your bike. It can be relatively expensive to do so—premiums tend to be approximately ten per cent of the value of the bike per year. But it is a major consolation that you can afford to replace your bike if it is stolen; sadly, a significant proportion of people who have a bicycle stolen stop cycling as a result. Some household insurance policies will cover a bicycle, up to a certain value. If insuring, do read the policy carefully, so that you are aware of exemptions and what you need to do to fulfil its conditions.

Lights

Lights are a legal and practical necessity. In the past, this was a drag because they tended to be heavy and unreliable. But thanks largely to LED technology, they are vastly improved. It used to be the case that the flashing LED-type light was not considered legal, but the ruling on this has changed. Most lights now have a flashing mode and a steady beam mode. It is up to you which you use, but especially for rear lights I believe the flashing mode is more eye-catching.

Light fantastic

For front lights, there are two choices—and it depends on what kind of light you need. If the object is simply to be seen by other road users, then a white LED type is perfectly adequate. This will not, however, cast much light for you to see by, so if your journey requires you to ride on roads without street-lighting where you actually need to light your own way, then you will need a more powerful lamp. You may wish to consider a halogen lamp, which throws good white light, but draws quite a lot of power. Another option is using a cluster of LED lights to create enough light. These lights will be more expensive than the minimal LED type. Often, because of their greater power demand, they involve a rechargeable battery unit. This is sensible from a cost and environmental point of view, but means the unit is heavier than an LED light running off two or three AAA batteries. In general, expect to pay £20-£40 ($35-$70) for a pair of lights. The fittings are usually relatively easy to install with just a screwdriver.

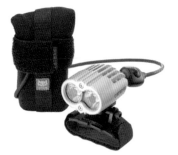
A powerful LED front light with a battery recharger.

A simple three LED front light.

A back light with five LEDs.

A few bright ideas

1. Ensure that your lights are fitted in such a way as to be clearly and fully visible, and not be obscured by, say, panniers.

2. Remember to remove them when you leave your bike locked up, or they will get stolen.

3. LED lights give remarkably long battery life, but it can be useful to carry a few spare batteries in a pocket of your bike bag or pannier—since it always seems to be at the least convenient moment that a battery goes flat.

Tools

Depending on where and what your journey is, it can be a very good idea to carry a few tools. If you are only using your bike to cycle to work or the shops, and know that you will never be more than mile or so from a bike shop, then perhaps you can dispense with this. But otherwise, as a minimum, you should have the wherewithal to repair a puncture, which is:

1. A mini pump

2. A spare inner tube

3. A set of tyre levers

A mini-pump is a hard way of pumping up your tyres if you have no other (much easier to keep a 'track' pump–the type that stands upright–at home), and is a very convenient way of making sure you are not utterly stranded by a puncture. The logic of a spare inner tube is that it is much easier simply to replace your punctured tube with an intact one than to attempt a roadside repair to the tube itself (see page 74 for further details). Tyre levers are just about the cheapest item you can buy from a bike shop, and you can't afford to be without a set. For the most part, these are the only tools you would ever need as a commuting cyclist. For travelling further afield, however, it can be a good idea to carry one of the compact tool kits available from bike shops. Light and ingeniously designed, these will make sure you get home even in the rare but not unheard-of event that your chain breaks out on the road.

For longer rides, where you may end up miles from anywhere, let alone a bike shop, the basic kit should be supplemented with:

1. A further spare innertube

2. Mini toolkit, including chain breaker

3. A puncture repair kit

Clothing

Below: a selection of the latest in outerwear technology from the Interbike Show in California. Photograph by Vaughn Trevisanut.

Whether you ride in purpose-made cycling apparel or in everyday clothes is purely a matter of preference and practicality. Whichever you do, though, it is advisable to invest in a good waterproof jacket. It is worth spending a lot on this one item, because what your money will buy you is a jacket that is not only waterproof but breathable. No waterproof jacket can ever really be breathable enough, but even the mildest exertion in a non-breathable impermeable will mean that you get almost as damp underneath as you would without any rain protection at all.

Gore-Tex is the leading brand, but there are similar fabrics that allow some water vapour to escape while preventing ingress of rain. This kind of waterproof jacket does not come cheap—expect to pay £80–£100 ($140-$180). The good news about making this investment, though, is that you will feel impelled to use your bike no matter what the weather forecast is—just to get your money's worth.

Choosing shoes

After this purchase, the next best buy in cycling apparel is a pair of cycling shoes. These do not need to be racing shoes with hi-tech clasps and buckles; it is possible to buy cycling-specific shoes that do a passable impression of ordinary trainers. The real point of getting a pair of cycling shoes is that it will enable you to use pedals you can clip your feet into. Slightly confusingly, these are still generally referred to as 'clipless' pedals—to distinguish them from the old-style toe clips that came right over the front of the shoe and included a leather strap with a buckle on the side.

Modern clipless pedals contain a binding system similar to ski bindings: you press your foot into the pedal, and to release, simply twist your foot out. The shoes themselves have a cleat that slots into the pedal's binding; these metal cleats are recessed so that you can walk normally in the shoes. Cycling shoes tend to have stiffer soles than normal shoes—purposely, since the more a shoe flexes with each pedal stroke, the more power is lost. The stiffness of the sole makes cycling shoes feel a little strange at first for walking in, but you soon become accustomed to it.

It takes just a couple of tries to master cycling with clipless pedals. Scarcely anyone trying them for the first time gets away without an embarrassing fall sideways when they come to a stop and can't get their foot out in time—but it usually only happens once. The value of being able to clip in to your pedals is that it makes pedalling much more efficient and, in fact, safer since your foot can't slip off the pedal if you get out of the saddle to speed up. It is possible to buy pedals that have a clip on one side, but are flat on the other—so that you can ride either with cycling shoes or ordinary shoes: a useful compromise.

Get shorties

Beyond a good Gore-Tex jacket and a practical pair of cycling shoes lies a world of lycra and nylon polyamide to be explored. For longer rides, a proper pair of cycling shorts is a very good idea—the padded insert (still sometimes called a 'chammy', since they used to be made from chamois leather) is there for a reason. The bib-type shorts, with straps over the shoulders, are generally more comfortable to wear than shorts with a drawstring at the waist. Hygiene is the golden rule with shorts: they should be washed after every use, or at least every day. Not to put too fine a point on it, the cyclist's crotch is a happy breeding ground for bacteria, and any encouragement to undesirable microbes is likely to lead to saddle sores and other uncomfortable problems. Bear in mind also that shorts are summer-wear. You always see a few hardy types cycling to work all winter in just a pair of shorts and a T-shirt, but this is not recommended: knee problems, for example, can be exacerbated by the cold.

Helmets

Helmets are a slightly vexed subject. In the UK (unlike, for instance, some states in Australia), there is no legal obligation to wear a bicycle helmet-except for racing, where helmet use is governed by sporting bodies. Many people voluntarily do wear a helmet on the public highway, and there is plenty of opinion, notably from doctors' and dentists' organisations, to support helmet-wearing. However, there is a vociferous minority point of view that argues that helmet use must remain voluntary only. Compulsory helmet use, the argument goes, would discourage many casual cyclists, particularly women cyclists, from riding. It would also be an infringement of personal freedom—the right not to wear a helmet, if you like.

On top of this, the anti-helmet lobby says the claims of helmet proponents that helmets save injuries and lives are not as solid as they may appear. There is some evidence that cyclists wearing helmets take more risks than non-helmet wearers: in other words, the fact that they feel protected and less vulnerable leads them to compensate by riding more recklessly.

The design of cycle helmets, it is also argued, makes them very easy to break. They are generally made of expanded polystyrene, with a thin plastic skin to protect the outer surface, and this in-built fragility means that their efficacy in the case of anything other than fairly low-impact incidents is challenged. Designers riposte that this is precisely the way helmets are meant to work—they are not intended to provide a cyclist protection against, say, a car travelling at 70 kilometres per hour. Instead, they are meant to save a cyclist from head injury in the case of a fall to the road surface at relatively low speeds (less than 50 kilometres per hour). Their design is such that they will only work for one such crash, since they are made to absorb the impact by the collapsing of their own structures.

The advocacy on both sides is extremely forthright, and both sides seem able to muster reams of statistics to support their respective cases, so one ventures into the pro/anti-helmet debate at one's own risk. All I would say is that, yes, helmet use should be a matter of personal conscience, but that my own choice is almost always to wear one. I have smashed one helmet in a crash, during a race, and I felt that it definitely saved me from a serious concussion or possibly worse—even if I have no scientific way of proving this assertion. My children wear helmets when they cycle, and again I would say that there have been several occasions when doing so has saved them from worse scrapes and knocks than the ones they got. But this, again, is anecdotal and subjective testimony. Common sense suggests that almost all of us will fall off our bikes occasionally and that wearing any kind of helmet is better than wearing none.

As far as buying a helmet is concerned, you are not going to get a tougher, longer-lasting helmet by spending more. Possibly the reverse, since the more expensive helmets tend to be lighter and more extensively vented. A perfectly good helmet can be had for £30 ($50). If you pay more, then it is either for performance or fashion (both perfectly good reasons in my book).

Make sure when you buy a helmet that it really is the right size: snug enough not to move around too easily, but not actually tight on your head. It's a really good idea to get the hang of adjusting the straps, since some unwanted 'play' always seems to occur eventually and it is important for the helmet to be fitted properly at all times if it's to work in an emergency. 'Properly fitted' also means that the helmet should sit forward on your head, its front rim almost down to your eyebrows. If you can see your hairline in the mirror (or where your hairline used to be, guys) under the helmet, you're not wearing it correctly and it may not help you in a crash.

There is an argument that the hard shell helmets now sometimes sold in bike shops but modelled on snowboarders' helmets afford greater protection. That may very well be so—they may survive a moderate knock when an ordinary bike helmet would need replacing. But these helmets tend to be much less ventilated, and so are pretty uncomfortable to wear in anything but very cool conditions.

Caring for your bike

Maintenance

The more you look after your bike, the more it will reward you with trouble-free riding. If you want to pay someone else to look after it, that's fine. Not everyone is a dab hand with allen keys and spanners, or wants to be. And bicycle grease is a pretty good disincentive. The first tip, therefore, if you are going to do some maintenance yourself is to get yourself a good barrier cream to protect your hands. The other essential ingredient is some of the eco-friendly solvent sold in bike shops—this is good for cleaning not only bike parts, but also your hands afterwards. Because it is water-soluble, it can usually be diluted in at least a 50:50 proportion and still be very effective.

Cleaning your bike is something no one will do if you don't. A bike put in for a full service will get some kind of cursory wipe-over, but mechanics are more likely to change parts and charge you for them than spend valuable working time scrubbing down the grubby bits of your pride-and-joy. So, even if you do no other maintenance, do this. The worst job of any bike-cleaning episode is the transmission. But it is also the most necessary.

Sins of transmission

The chain, which should always be sufficiently lubricated, inevitably accumulates dust and grit. The problem with this is that, over time, this black greasy gunk begins to act less and less as a lubricant and more and more as a kind of improvised abrasive. That grit is gradually but methodically grinding away at the teeth of the chainring and sprockets. If you do not clean your chain at all, it is perfectly possible, through normal use, to trash a chainring over the course of one winter. But keep it clean and it will last much longer; easily several years if you are conscientious.

Chain reaction

You can save yourself the trouble of cleaning the chain at least twice a year by simply replacing it. The chain is one of the cheapest parts on your bike, but if you do not change it regularly it will mean you have to change a much more expensive part such as the cassette. Chains wear relatively quickly, if imperceptibly to the naked eye, by 'stretching'—that is, the distance between the bushes gradually grows until the entire chain is half a link or so longer than it was when first fitted. This doesn't sound much, but it is enough for the links no longer to fit so snugly into the teeth of the sprockets. Combine a worn chain with the sandpaper effect of a dirty chain and very soon you have a set of sprockets so reamed out that a new chain will no longer fit on them at all. If you change the chain but then find that it jumps disconcertingly across the sprockets when you apply pedal pressure, this is what has happened. Unfortunately, it is then too late for just a new chain; you need a new cassette too.

The nitty-gritty

There are chain-cleaning kits that can be bought from bike shops. But the most effective (and ultimately painless) way of cleaning a chain is to remove it entirely with a chain-breaking tool. These are easy enough to use with a bit of practice, but it is a good idea to get a friend to show you the first time, if possible. It is also worth buying the best quality tool, because chain-breaking is made much easier with a precision tool. Just use the tool to push one rivet out (but only so far that the end remains fixed in the furthest plate, not right out altogether), and then place the chain in a jar or tin with a lid and cover with undiluted bike grease solvent. Shake and leave; the solvent will do the rest–a few hours, or overnight, is sufficient. Then scrub any remaining grease away with an old brush, wash off the solvent with a detergent, and rinse. Dry the chain as thoroughly as possible by pulling through an old rag (you do not want rust to set in). A car-washing detergent (containing wax polymers) is probably a better bet than simple washing-up liquid.

Totally riveting

Then re-thread the chain through the derailleurs (you have to use the end without the protruding rivet for this), and line up the two ends of the chain so that the rivet is over its original hole. Use the chain-breaker in reverse (as a 'chain-maker'). Be careful not to push the rivet too far, which is easily done. The final step is that you will find that this re-made link is very stiff; it must be loosened before you are finished. Sometimes this can be done simply by flexing the chain laterally, but more than likely you will need to use the chain-breaker to push the rivet back the other way a fraction to loosen it up. Again, it is a procedure quickly learnt just by watching someone else do it. Once the chain is back on the bike and running freely, remember to reapply lubricant evenly. For summer use, especially, the lightest possible synthetic lube is a good idea. Generally speaking, the heavier the oil, the quicker it picks up dirt. That said, a light oil may not be enough to protect your chain from rust in the winter months. It is a compromise.

Lube tube

For a really thorough job that will leave your bike purring with contentment, taking the chain off is the opportunity to get at the chainrings and sprockets and give them a good clean also. An old tooth brush and your eco-friendly solvent is all you need. Then wash off with soapy water. On modern bikes, the important bearings on the wheels and at the cranks are usually well sealed, so you can afford to be fairly enthusiastic with the rinsing without having to worry about harming the bike. Note, though, that even the best-sealed bearing will not stand a direct blast from a jet-wash–although this is a perfectly legitimate way to clean a really muddy mountain bike. After a thorough wash and dry, remember to lubricate not only the chain but other moving parts, preferably with a light spray oil like WD40 that replaces moisture: the derailleur mechanisms, brake pivots, brake and gear levers, cable housings and so on can all use this treatment. It is best to wipe excess lube away as you go, or it will soon attract a film of greasy dust.

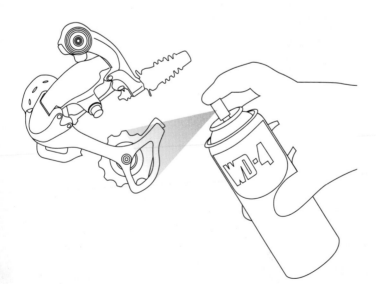

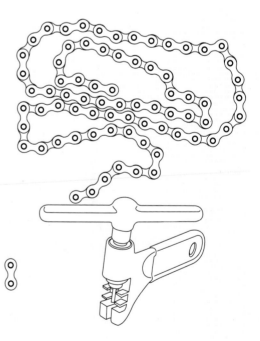

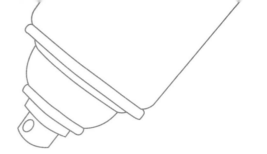

Maintenance: other basics

The main areas of wear on a bike are brake pads and cables. Cables tend to stretch soon after fitting. This is normal and they soon bed down, but it may mean that brakes and gears need a small adjustment within weeks of a new cable being fitted or in the case of it being a brand new bike. Most cable-operated brake and gear systems have small tension adjusters fitted either at the brake or at the lever or at both. Altering the tension on the cable is simply a matter of screwing one of these adjusters in or out a little at a time, until the desired tension is restored. Very often, if your gears have stopped working so well (so that a gear change, either up or down, does not result in a smooth change), this is all it takes to restore neatly indexed gearing.

Take a brake

In the case of brakes, be aware that there are other reasons for loss of braking force besides cable stretch. Brake cables need periodic adjustment also because, as brake blocks wear at the rim, this means that the brake calipers have to travel further to produce a good contact with the rim. Depending on make and compound, brake blocks can last a very long time, but with heavy use in wet conditions, they can also wear surprisingly quickly. This is something to keep an eye on. Replacing brake blocks is certainly a task that can easily be done at home, and usually just needs an allen key (a decent-quality set of allen keys of different sizes is a good investment). But it does require some patience and skill to align the new pads correctly on the rim. The easiest way of doing this is to fit the new pad approximately but without tightening its fixing bolt fully, so that you can still nudge it. Then operate the brake so that the pad makes a firm contact with the rim. When you have the pad correctly positioned on the braking surface of the rim, then tighten fully, and finally check that the position has remained correct.

In the case of modern disc brake designs, especially the type that is hydraulically operated (not by cable), it may be best to take the job back to the shop where you bought the bike. Or refer carefully to manufacturers' instructions, if you want to attempt maintenance yourself.

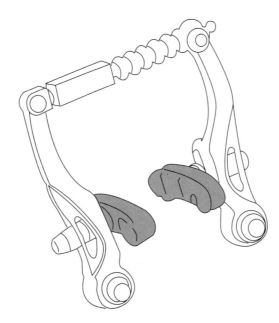

Nuts and bolts matters

In general, be careful not to over-tighten bolts and nuts on your bike—most components are manufactured in light alloys rather than hardened steel and do not take kindly to huge torque forces. It is a good habit to apply a little grease to the contact surfaces of all nuts and bolts as you are doing maintenance on your bike. They will come off much easier next time; otherwise, there is some risk, especially with periodic exposure to water (either from rain or through washing), of parts that have not been greased 'cold-welding' themselves together. The classic example is the seatpost (the part that joins the saddle to the frame). It is highly advisable to remove the entire seatpost from the frame, clean the shaft and regrease, at least once a year to prevent the seatpost freezing in place. "How to remove a stuck-solid seatpost" is a staple of cycling website chatrooms: it involves a hacksaw blade, a couple of hours and sore fingers—a procedure to be avoided at all costs. The only exception to the regreasing rule is if you have a carbon-fibre seatpost—these should not be greased as they will simply not stay in place if lubricated. But the drill of removing them from time to time and wiping clean and dry the contact surfaces is still a good one. I didn't and now have a perfectly good and rather pricey carbon seatpost stuck in a broken old steel frame.

Wheel time

The only other issue of wear-and-tear to look out for on your bike is any sign of damage to the rims of your wheels. If your bike has disc brakes, this type of wear is virtually eliminated. But if your bike has conventional brakes, then you should know that the rims themselves get worn, as well as the brake pads. Particularly on dirty winter roads, pads can collect grit which rapidly scours the braking surfaces (another good reason to keep your bike reasonably clean and maintained through the winter). If the rim becomes deeply grooved or pitted, it may be time to get a professional opinion and, possibly, replace the rims (most wheels can be re-built straightforwardly enough). You do not want to get to the stage where the rim wall becomes so thin that the tyre pressure alone buckles it out of shape—by this point, the whole wheel would be at risk of potentially catastrophic collapse. Modern wheels are very strong and robust, and may go almost indefinitely without needing to be trued. But it is common enough for wheels to 'go out of true', that is, to develop a slight wobble or kink which is visible from behind as they rotate. With most designs, it is possible to correct this at home by adjusting the tension of the spokes. But this is a relatively skilled job, and one best learned at a bicycle maintenance course. If you do not have time for this, then it is a relatively quick and inexpensive job for the mechanic at your local bike shop.

Puncture repair

If you do no other repair or maintenance on your bike, this is the one skill really worth mastering—if only because it is so inconvenient not to be able to do it. It is an observable fact that punctures occur much more easily when it has been raining. (This has something to do with the physics of how small shards of glass or flint get picked up by the tyre and then work their way in through the tyre compound in the wet.) This means that the chances of your being stranded with a flat tyre on a cold damp night are, unfortunately, greater than on a nice, clear, dry morning. Given this scenario, being able to effect a quick puncture repair and be on your way again is a near-essential capability.

Rule one:

Do not repair the puncture. Instead, just replace the inner tube. Pump the tyre back up and take the damaged inner tube with you, so that you can repair it in the comfort of your own home and at your leisure. The essential roadside kit, then, is a spare inner tube, a set of three tyre levers and a pump or inflation device (bike shops sell small canisters of compressed gas for this purpose).

Rule two:

You need to take the wheel off. Bear in mind that to repair a puncture this way, you do need to be able to remove the wheel fully from the frame. If you have quick release skewers, this is simple enough, but with a rear wheel puncture it is a good idea to drop the chain onto the lowest gear first (that is, the smallest, bottom cog)—this makes it much easier to relocate the wheel when you are putting it back.

Rule three:

Ease the tyre off one side only. Once you have got the wheel off, then use the tyre levers to get one side (only) of the tyre off the rim, so that you can access the inner tube. There is no need to take the whole tyre off in order to get the inner tube off.

Rule four:

Find what made the puncture. Before you remove the inner tube entirely, it is vital to establish, if possible, where the puncture is. The easiest way of discovering this is to inflate the inner tube a little while it is still in situ. A gentle hissing will generally tell you where to look ('slow punctures' too slow to be seen and heard are actually quite unusual). The importance of this is that you then want to match up where the hole in the inner tube is with where the tyre was punctured—for the simple reason that very often whatever made the puncture in the first place is still stuck in the tyre. To repair a puncture with your spare inner tube and set off again, only to be brought to a halt a couple of hundred metres down the road with another puncture in the very same spot is, shall we say, a pretty deflating experience.

Rule five:

If the tyre is badly cut, try to patch it.
Occasionally, a tyre will have been badly
cut by a piece of glass, so that there is a
perceptible hole on the inside of the tyre.
Even if the shard is no longer there, this
can be a problem since an inner tube
under pressure may force its way into
that small hole and fairly soon cause
another puncture. If the tyre is badly cut
in many places, then it may mean that it
is time to replace it. But in the meantime
it is a good idea to patch the hole before
replacing a new inner tube. On long rides,
it is best to carry a few small strips of
gaffer's tape (they can be temporarily
adhered to your spare inner tube) for
this patching job.

Rule six:

Do not use the levers again to get the tyre back on.
Replacing the tyre, after you have fitted the new inner
tube, is easiest done if the inner tube has a little air in
it—just a little, to give it shape. Sometimes the fit of the
tyre can be very tight over the rim of the wheel. Use of
tyre levers to get a tyre back on is best avoided because
it is so easy to pinch the inner tube and puncture it with
the levers when doing this. But sometimes, use of the
levers is practically impossible to avoid, in which case all
you can do is your best to avoid pinching the inner tube
between the lever and the rim as you pull the tyre back
on. Finally, it is often easier to pump up a tyre before you
put it back in the forks or rear dropouts—but only as long
as it will be easy to get an inflated tyre back in past the
brake pads. Think of it as a good workout for your arms:
cyclists tend to neglect their arms.

The gentle art of patching tubes

When it comes to repairing the inner tube, the best kind of repair kit is the type that gives you a flat sheet of patch rubber from which to cut your own patches. (And there is no reason why an inner tube should not have a long life and collect numerous patches.) Ready-made patches are fine, but are often larger than they need to be—and more difficult to get to adhere as a result. The inner tube surface around the puncture needs to be completely clean and dry; roughening up the area gently with a piece of sandpaper does no harm—and helps as the friction will warm it up. The rubber solution or cement works by acting as a partial solvent and 'melting' the surface of the rubber so that it forms a bond with the patch. This is easier to achieve if you are working in a warm, dry place. It is also important to allow the solution—spread in a thin, even layer around the puncture—to 'go off' or dry before you try to apply the patch. This generally takes three or four minutes, but should ensure that you obtain an almost instantaneous and solid bond. It is a simple enough procedure—but so much easier to get right at home than by the roadside when everything is wet and your fingers are numb. Levers, mini-pump and spare inner: never leave home without them!

Inflationary pressures

If all this sounds nightmarish, don't fret: the good news is that most modern tyres are exceptionally puncture-resistant. Look for the word 'Kevlar' when you're buying—it's the same stuff they make bullet-proof vests out of. The best tyres on this score will not be the lightest or the fastest, but unless you are a sports cyclist, this hardly matters. Take the advice of bike shop staff, choose a tough, durable tyre, and you may well go from one year to the next without any punctures at all. With luck.

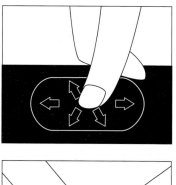
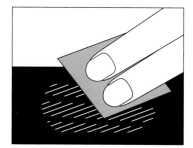

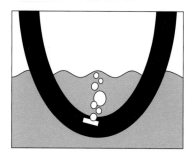

When your mind and body are attuned to the machine, you feel like you could ride forever.

Helen Cooney/UK

Below: Dunedin, New Zealand: "Baldwin Street is officially the steepest road in the world. Those who cycle up it get a certificate. I tried three times, all with the same result.... Coming down was fun though!"

Helen Cooney, a Chief Inspector with Merseyside Police, in Liverpool, England, has always been a keen cyclist. At the age of 19, she cycled through the Pyrenees with her cousin, and has ridden with various organisations and on numerous tours, including L'Etape, since then. However, she has never had the speed, nor the competitive inclination to cycle professionally, and so, at the age of 39, she set herself a very different type of challenge: to cycle around the world.

Taking a year's leave from her job, she planned her journey meticulously. In fact it took her over a year to properly prepare. She decided to follow the summer, and so travelled eastwards, choosing a route that took in the highlights of both Eastern and Western cultures. Athens, Cairo, Delhi, Bangkok and New York were top of her list as were major sights like the Taj Mahal and the Grand Canyon. Looking back on her travels she has countless observations about attitudes towards cycling in various countries:

In Holland, the cyclist is king. They have their own network of well-maintained signposted cycle lanes and tracks. I spent a week in the country hardly touching a road. Bliss! ... In Asia, despite the apparent chaos on the roads, it is actually quite easy and safe to cycle because most of the traffic (the rickshaws, trishaws, carts and tuk-tuks) is actually travelling at a cyclists' pace (that is an average of 18.6 kilometres per hour in my case).

Above left: Bulgaria: "... a lovely country to cycle in."

Above right: New Mexico: "As high as it gets. Nothing compares to the thrill of reaching a summit under your own steam, and this one is one of the all-time greats."

Helen chose to take a steel-framed bicycle, for the simple reason that should anything go wrong, or if the frame were to break, it could be easily fixed, no matter where in the world she found herself. She used clipless pedals and installed butterfly framed handlebars, so that she could vary her cycling position, thus reducing pressure on her back. Her decision to travel on her own is not one she regrets:

Cycling is actually quite a private affair. Its success depends upon how your body reacts with the bike and the environment on a given day, and this can change frequently. A good day, a bad day, a good few hours, some time feeling rotten.... Trying to manage this in a round-the-world schedule is difficult enough; but to find a compatible companion, one who will want to cycle the same distance at the same speed day after day, is almost impossible.

She's now back with the police force, cycling a 30 kilometre commute to work and back every day. Her memories of her trip are fond ones:

For every moment of exhaustion, rainy skies, brutal headwinds, dangerous traffic and general pain and unhappiness that every cyclist encounters, there is also a moment of sheer ecstasy; when the road is right, the weather is perfect, the breeze behind you; when your body and mind are totally attuned to the machine and you feel like you could ride forever. These are the moments that make cycling worthwhile, and the reason why so many cyclists, myself included, are cyclists for life.

Cycling and the city

One of the slogans I like from the Critical Mass movement is "We are traffic". Critical Mass began in 1992 in San Francisco; it involved cyclists simply getting together for a monthly ride through city streets as a way of asserting their collective right to exist, and to celebrate cycling as a socially responsible and environmentally benign alternative form of transport. The idea soon caught on and in the years since, Critical Mass has become a global phenomenon, with hundreds of monthly rides in cities all over the world.

Of course, "We are traffic" is an assertion that only needs to be made in contexts where cyclists are regarded as marginal or a nuisance. In many towns and cities in northern Europe (particularly in Germany, The Netherlands, Denmark and Sweden), for cyclists to gather and insist that "We are traffic" would merely seem like a statement of the blindingly obvious. In many of those places, urban areas, trips by bike comprise ten to 15 per cent—even as high as 25 per cent in some places—of all journeys. Where cycling has this much 'modal share', as the transport planners call it, cyclists have truly achieved a critical mass.

What cycle use at such densities achieves is a complete change in priorities on the roads. Drivers are used to seeing cyclists everywhere, and are therefore more competent at driving in proximity to cyclists. They also expect to travel at slower speeds, and this may often, in fact, be mandated by lower speed limits. In London, for instance, this effect of increased cycle use leading to increased relative safety has dramatically proved true: in the past two years, cycle use has grown by 50 per cent in

Above: a mixed-use bicycle/pedestrian path in Long Beach, California.

central London, yet—despite the greater number of cyclists on the road—casualties have fallen over the same period in absolute terms by 40 per cent. At some point, the objective truth that cycling is getting safer really does spill over into people's subjective sense that cycling in a busy city is maybe not as scary and dangerous as they used to think.

In many European cities, whereas previously cyclists were channelled by the motor traffic into a narrow corridor at the edge of the road, now they either have broad, extensive cycle paths on useful arterial routes, or they share priority with pedestrians in central areas where vehicular traffic is prohibited. This is another big change underway. The old orthodoxy of traffic engineers and transport planners was that cyclists and pedestrians were mutually antagonistic road users and needed to be segregated. Thus town centres were often pedestrianised in a way that specifically excluded bikes, along with cars. But at some point someone threw a philosophical switch on this issue. The new way is for private cars still to be excluded (possibly from larger areas in urban centres), but for pedestrian areas to be designated as shared use. The theory is that where pedestrians and cyclists have equal rights and expect to find each other in the street, they make allowances for each other. At a stroke, the culture of 'mutual antagonism' is abolished.

All of these changes require political will. In Germany, for instance, the decision was taken by local governments 15 or 20 years ago to spend heavily on cycling as part of a sustainable transport policy. The figures of ten per cent and more modal share for cycling are a direct result of that investment—a spend per capita of population of five, even ten, times what local authorities in the UK spend on cycling.

Local politicians have to be persuaded that moving people out of cars and onto public transport and bicycles will be good for their constituents. Boosting cycle use does challenge the supremacy of the motoring lobby—and most voters are motorists. But what European cities have proved in ever greater numbers is that the slogan of 'sustainability' is not only about having a green policy and being 'environmentally correct', but is also about making their cities better places to live and work—which ultimately attracts investment and builds the local economy. In other words, there is a growing realisation that a sound business case can be mounted for making cities more cycle-friendly. It is no coincidence that the towns with some of the highest figures for cycle use in the UK—such as Cambridge, York, Kingston—are also among the most prosperous towns in the country.

Above: a cyclist overtakes a virtually static row of cars. Photograph by Metin Alsanjak.

So much for what cycling does for a city. But what does a city do for the cyclist? Riding a bike in the city can be a frustrating, difficult, uncomfortable, even frightening business, but it can also be a superbly elevating, wonderfully satisfying experience. First off, cycling is probably the most reliable form of urban transport there is (very occasional mishaps, such as punctures, excepted). In some cities, of course, driving is convenient and comfortable, but in very few places is it completely reliable—roadworks, accidents, rush hour congestion, even just a rainy day can all add time to a journey. It has been found that motorists typically underestimate how long a given journey by car will take by about 50 per cent (partly because they do not count the full door-to-door duration, including the time taken to find a parking space and walk from there to the final destination). In other words, they usually quote the best-case scenario—the quickest time they've ever done a given journey, their 'ideal' time, as the regular figure. By fascinating contrast, if you ask the same people how long a particular journey would take by bike, they overestimate by a similar factor (that is, 50 per cent).

Not a mistake any cyclist would make, of course. One of the great pleasures of using a bike in town is that you almost always know the length of time any given journey will take, down to a few minutes either way. There is never any reason why a cyclist should be late—unless he or she doesn't leave enough time for the journey. And with that reliability comes a tremendous sense of empowerment and independence. You do not have to rely on anyone else to get you from A to B. You are never the helpless victim of someone else's problem, breakdown or crisis, or just of plain bad service. Nor do you need to allow extra time to allow for delays on public transport or for traffic congestion if driving. On a bike, you are not beholden to anyone—which is a great feeling.

Cycling and the mind

Another distinct aspect of cycling is the way that a cyclist apprehends his or her environment. Unlike a motorist, who is cut off from their immediate surroundings, cyclists fully experience the sights, sounds and smells of the world they are pedalling through, and are able to cover much more ground at much faster pace than any pedestrian. Where a pedestrian in London, for example, can cover a page of an A-Z, a cyclist can link up several pages at a time. Knowing where you are and how to get around has so much to do with a person's sense of ownership of the city. The cyclist is the ultimate realisation of the *flâneur*, what the poet Charles Baudelaire called "the passionate spectator", the person who travels through a city with the eye of an artist, observing everything, part of the flow of the urban bustle. Baudelaire's idea of the *flâneur* was a type of intelligent, idle drifter whose existence in Paris was threatened by the *dirigiste* logic of Haussmann's boulevards. He might have been surprised, then, to find his notion surviving and even thriving through the twentieth century.

First, the German intellectual and theorist of Modernism, Walter Benjamin, took up the cause of *flânerie*. He defined this city-wanderer as one "who goes botanising on the asphalt", someone in whom "the joy of watching is triumphant". In other words, *flânerie* is a sophisticated term for the simple pleasure of people-watching and a particularly unfocused and aimless form of tourism. This activity was further refined, mystified even, by the Situationists, for whom the idea of the '*dérive*'—a close cousin of the *flâneur's* ironic stroll—was a central principle of their theories of 'psychogeography'. As one of the Situationist International's key architects, Guy Debord, defined it: "In a *dérive* one or more persons during a certain period drop their usual motives for movement and action, their relations, their work and leisure activities, and let themselves be drawn by the attractions of the terrain and the encounters they find there." The distinction between the Situationist *dérive* and Benjaminian '*flânerie*' is that, for Debord and friends, the 'drifting' is not random but purposive, albeit obscurely so. The *dériviste* surrenders himself to the secret, hidden currents of power, interest and desire that, they held, run through the urban environment. The *dérive* is therefore "a technique of transient passage through varied ambiences" in order to reveal a city's occult psychogeography.

These are rather abstract and fanciful concepts, but they do seem to me to relate to the counter-cultural way in which a cyclist progresses through an urban environment. Because they can go where most traffic cannot, cyclists tend to use back streets and unconventional routes, accessing parts of the city that are screened off from the majority of people. The mental map of the different neighbourhoods in a city and how they relate to one another is totally different for a cyclist than the one held by someone who relies on underground travel or on the major arterial routes that most motorists stick to. So much more of the history of a city's development and its patterns of poverty and wealth are visible to the cyclist. A simple illustration of this is to visit an unfamiliar city and explore it by bicycle; there is no better way to establish a rudimentary knowledge of its layout and character. "The city is the realisation of that ancient dream of humanity, the labyrinth", wrote Benjamin. Travelling by bicycle allows these secrets and puzzles to be unlocked; it makes you fully a citizen of the polis.

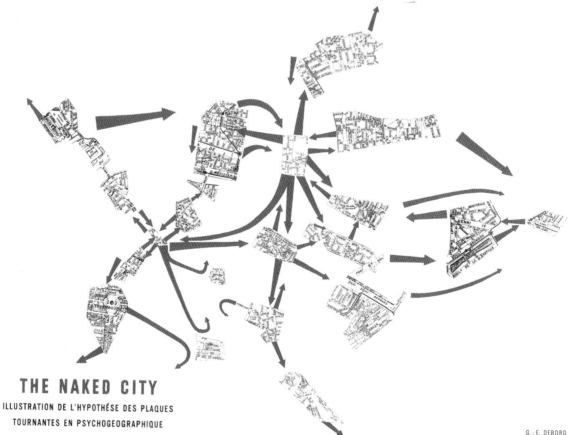

THE NAKED CITY

ILLUSTRATION DE L'HYPOTHÉSE DES PLAQUES
TOURNANTES EN PSYCHOGEOGRAPHIQUE

G.-E. DEBORD

Cycling and the body

Cycling certainly exercises the brain and expands the life of the mind. The bicycle is an ideal place to do the sort of unconscious, 'alpha state' thinking that, among others, the great jazz saxophonist Stan Getz revered as the fount of true creativity. Any repetitive, rhythmic physical activity, which relies on a certain human automatism, can work, but cycling is particularly good. Thoughts grow larger, problems get solved, ideas are born, as you pedal along.

Not only, but also... for cycling is an ideal instance of the Roman proverb '*mens sana in corpore sano*' (a healthy mind in a healthy body). Cycling is, after all, a physical activity–as well as a matter of intellectual enquiry and philosophical attitude. It is, simply, exercise. It makes us breathe deeper and our hearts beat faster, pumping oxygen-rich blood around the body. It burns calories, especially the ones we get from the carbohydrates and fats in our diet. Among the many health benefits of cycling, I read recently in a newspaper article is that it is good for our skin and makes us look younger. Who knew? Forget botox, darling, just ride a bike!

One commonly quoted bike fact is that a regular cyclist (meaning a commuter, not a sports cyclist) has on average the fitness of a person ten years younger. Cycling is good for you because it is perfect, no-impact aerobic exercise. For most people, if they cycle to and from work, then that's their recommended 30 minutes a day of exercise done right there—no expensive lunchtime dash to gym needed. It is also appropriate exercise for people of all ages because your weight is supported as you cycle—it can be as energetic a cardio-vascular workout as running, but there is much less wear and tear on joints.

Another benefit of cycling, along with many forms of exercise, is that it is a great antidote for stress and anxiety. For similar reasons, exercise is now often advised for people suffering from depression, as it stimulates the release of brain chemicals known as endorphins—the 'feel good' opiates that provide a natural 'high', causing the sense of well-being you get after brisk exercise. So there turns out to be a virtuous circle here: the body being healthy helps keeps the mind healthy too. Or is that a virtuous cycle?

Pollution

What you need to know

But, of course, not everything in the garden can be rosy. One potential downside of cycling is that, while it is an intrinsically healthy activity, the environment in which you are obliged to cycle may not be quite so wholesome as you are, and although your ecological credentials as a cyclist are impeccable, you still have to breathe in everyone else's pollution.

Pedestrians also suffer, of course, from pollution caused by traffic, but there is some evidence that as you move further away from the vehicles themselves, the adverse impact falls off rapidly—even the width of a pavement can make a difference—when you're looking right down the tailpipe of a car, bus or lorry, however, it's another matter. While cleaner fuels and catalytic converters have helped reduce the toxicity of exhaust fumes over recent years (lead, for instance, has largely been eliminated as a petrol additive; and the sulphur content of diesel has been cut), petrol still contains benzene, a known carcinogen.

Probably the greatest threat to cyclists' health, however, comes from the sub-microscopic soot particles, known as PM10s, produced by diesel combustion. These are tiny, sticky particles of partially burnt hydro-carbons that contain a cocktail of chemicals including several known carcinogens, and are so small that they can be carried deep into the lungs. No one knows the long-term consequences of prolonged and habitual exposure to traffic pollution generally and PM10s specifically. Presumably it will take an epidemiological survey of lung cancer and related respiratory diseases in cyclists many years from now to determine what effect there may have been.

Some cyclists like to use masks to protect themselves from environmental pollution. In theory, this seems like a sensible idea if you are particularly concerned about the issue. Unfortunately, the evidence is that few, if any, of these masks are all that effective. Only activated charcoal masks can strip out from the surrounding atmosphere nasty gases such as sulphur dioxide and nitrous oxide—simple filters let these substances straight through. You would hope that filters would catch some of the soot particles, but sadly it does not seem to be the case. Either the particles themselves are so small (the PM10s are so-called because they are no more than ten microns in diameter) that they can pass through most filters, or the masks themselves are insufficiently close-fitting—so that the majority of the air breathed in by the cyclist is simply sucked in at the sides, rather than passing through the filter

Below: a Respro City mask, which uses charcoal filteration technology and a system of valves to make breathing easier.

itself. Added to this the fact that most masks are an uncomfortable encumbrance—and certainly very hot to wear in summer—makes them hard to recommend.

There are a couple small crumbs of comfort. Firstly, research has shown that motorists trapped in their cars tend to be breathing worse, more polluted air than pedestrians or cyclists. This is not great news for anyone, of course, except arguably for fans of poetic justice. A more significant (and less churlish) fact to celebrate is that, in the larger scheme of things, any health damage caused by exposure to pollution— pollution to which you would partly be exposed by whatever means you chose to travel—is more than offset by the health benefits of cycling. In other words, you are so much more likely to avoid, say, heart disease by cycling than risk dying of lung cancer as the (as yet not ascertained) result of PM10 exposure that you should stick to biking. The truth is that, once bitten by the cycling bug, it is hard not to stick to it. Just hold your breath when you're riding behind a dirty diesel, if you can.

Additional benefits

Cycle campaigners have often staged events such as 'the commuter challenge' where several people are dispatched from a suburban location to a central one—mimicking a typical commuting journey of perhaps six or seven miles—by different means: car, bus, underground and bicycle. The bike invariably comes out a clear winner. Motorcycles and mopeds are the only form of transport to rival the speed through traffic of a bike, being generally faster except in very heavy traffic on narrow streets (where perhaps a bicycle can get through gaps too slim for a motorbike). But motorcyclists have to hold in their heads a map of where all the designated parking zones are—and some may be quite a distance from their desired destination. Motorcyclists also have to carry or find some safe way to lock up a large, heavy helmet; and many choose to wear protective clothing—waterproofs and leathers—which tend to be cumbersome to move around in off the bike.

Going by bicycle makes multiple stops easy and convenient. Parking is almost always at hand within a few metres, and stopping time is only as long as it takes to lock up. And this convenience factor is closely related to another crucial aspect of cycle use—its sociability. My experience, in fact, is that cyclists could be a good deal more sociable towards each other. Brief pleasant exchanges while waiting at the lights do occur, but sadly not as often as that strange business of studious mutual ignoring that you might more readily expect among public transport passengers. This phenomenon may be worst not only in England, as opposed to other European countries, but also specifically in London, where people feel safer if they pursue a policy of non-engagement with strangers (even strangers on bikes). But what can be said is that the bicycle always provides the potential at least for human contact and social interaction. Chris Carlsson, one of the original founders of the Critical Mass movement, notes that one of the pleasures and advantages of going by bike in San Francisco is that it enables him to pull over and say hello whenever he spots an acquaintance on the street. Among recreational cyclists getting out of the city at the weekend, it is customary to acknowledge another cyclist passing with a nod or wave.

Bike-friendly employers

So, environmentally friendly, beneficial to mind and body, speedy, reliable and sociable... what's not to like? Surely if the bicycle became the main means of transport to and from work, it would make for both happier employers and employees. But there are a few things holding people back from turning to the bicycle as their main means of transport—things like security, hygiene and safety. Whilst safety concerns may be beyond an employers control, there are certain ways in which employers can make commuting by bicycle that much easier.

Probably the single most important measure for employers who want to encourage cycle use among their employees and visitors is the provision of secure, covered parking. Covered parking is important because a significant number of employees will be put off if their bike has to live out in all weathers, and if they always have to wipe down the saddle after rain before they can ride home. Secure speaks for itself: bike parking which is vulnerable to thieves, and from which bikes actually go missing, is entirely useless—any regular bike user would be forced to find some alternative parking. Secure means protected either by effective fencing, or by CCTV, or by security guard, or by swipe-card (or similar) access only—or, ideally, some combination of any or all of these. CCTV alone, for example, is not a sufficient deterrent—a thief only needs to be wearing a baseball cap and hooded top and work quickly to be more or less immune.

In general, company cycle parking needs as much protection as company car parking gets. It is estimated that each car parking space costs companies about £2,000 ($3,500) a year to maintain. Since a single car parking space can accommodate parking for up to five bikes, there is a considerable potential cost benefit to companies if they can convert car parking to bike parking, cut their overall space requirement and reduce this overhead. In London, for example, Transport for London operates an incentive scheme for employers by offering free cycle parking stands. The deal also offers matching funding for businesses to install other cyclist-friendly infrastructures such as changing facilities, lockers and showers. Discounted bikes are also available for 'pool' cycles—that is, a number of bikes owned and kept by the company that are available for use by employees who need to travel locally on company business.

Other local authorities have developed further ideas, such as encouraging employers to pay a bicycle mileage allowance (just as they would a car mileage allowance) for bicycle use for business purposes. Some enlightened employers may even offer cycle training and bike maintenance sessions.

Below: a simple covered shed provides
protection from the weather and
basic security.

The government's green transport plan also now enables employees
to lease a bike from their employer, and eventually purchase it tax-free.
The scheme is identical to the successful Home Computing Initiative
(HCI): the employer 'buys' the bike and any related accessories (lights,
locks, etc.), then the employee pays back the employer over a period of
12 to 18 months, all the while riding the bike. The repayments are made
before tax and national insurance, and when VAT rebates are taken
into account, most employees will have saved 40 to 50 per cent on the
retail price of the new bike. Once the lease expires (or the loan repaid,
whichever way you prefer to look at it), the employee becomes the
owner of the bike. Formerly, firms wishing to participate in the scheme
were required to obtain a Consumer Credit Licence to do so, but this
regulation has now been waived for bikes (and accessories) up to a value
of £1,000 ($1,700)—removing a significant obstacle for small employers.

With regards to hygiene concerns, some larger employers provide
changing rooms with showers and in many places grants are available
to install such facilities. Even if you can't shower, it is possible for most
people to 'freshen up' and change into a smarter set of clothes they
keep at work. With a bit of planning and preparation, you can arrive at
a business meeting by bike without looking a complete scruff. The best
tip is to allow a bit of extra time for the journey, so that you can cycle in a
leisurely manner and avoid working up a sweat.

Cycle parking

If employers are waking up to the benefits of a cycling workforce, so are local authorities waking up to the requirements of cyclists. Many local authorities are installing large numbers of cycle parking places, a relatively easy but important improvement in cycling infrastructure. The most common type of parking is the 'Sheffield stand'—a simple upturned U-bend of heavy-gauge steel, either bolted to or sunk into the pavement. This allows easy and secure locking on either side. There is increasing understanding among town planners and engineers that to encourage cycling, parking needs to be placed within 50 metres of popular destinations.

Of course, street furniture provides plenty of opportunities for parking—but there are pitfalls. Some businesses, for instance, object to bikes being chained to railings on their property. Equally, parking meters can seem convenient for cyclists, but can obstruct motorists from accessing their vehicle. Lamp posts and signage posts would seem to be useful for locking bikes to, but care has to be taken that a locked bike cannot simply be lifted up and off such posts—it does happen. The major drawback with locking bikes to any kind of street furniture—purpose-built or otherwise—is lack of security. Your bike is only as safe as your lock is effective. A secondary drawback is that your bike is, of course, open to the weather.

Many schools are now getting grants to put in covered bike sheds. These are of a good modern design, often covered in perspex so that they are transparent, which improves security—even if it does not provide such a good place to go to smoke. Some employers and local authorities are also installing secure locker-style parking for bikes. These are more expensive and occupy more space (although this is minimised by requiring the bike to be stored 'upright', with the front wheel elevated), but they perform very effectively the dual task of keeping bikes both dry and safe. Other local authorities are experimenting with converting some parking spaces in town centre multi-storey car parks to bike-parking places. Potentially, this can offer reasonably convenient and more secure parking to cyclists.

As a growing trend, many local authorities produce maps of cycle routes, which include details of special parking facilities. It is worth checking out your local government website for information; failing that, try contacting your local cycle campaigning group for further details.

Cycle routes

Over time, cycle routes have improved enormously. It is partly a matter of quantity—the more miles of dedicated cycle lanes and marked routes there are, the more they link up and provide useful and convenient ways of getting around an urban area. In the early days of cycle routes, there were so many examples of bad infrastructure—routes that started and finished in a disjointed, seemingly pointless manner—that the whole project struggled to make headway. Cyclists tended to scorn these half-cocked measures; often, they seemed worse than useless, and just a con to get cyclists out of the way of motorists.

But that has really changed: the routes have become more and more practical and user-friendly. Groups such as the UK-based sustainable transport charity, Sustrans and local cycling campaigns have produced excellent maps of cycle routes, as the network has expanded and filled in. It has taken time and effort to learn from the mistakes of the past, and to keep up momentum in the face of often sceptical local government officers. The degree of technical knowledge about how to install effective cycling infrastructure has grown enormously; and the links between traffic engineers, transport officers and cycling NGOs are now in place, ensuring that best practice gets shared around.

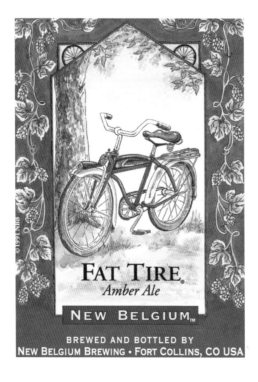

How to stay safe on your bike

Below: a poster by Transport for London promoting safe cycling.

The perception that cycling is unsafe is probably the most commonly cited reason for people not to use a bike. In fact, cycling is statistically safer per mile travelled than walking. Cycling casualties have been falling consistently over recent years, down by a third over the past decade. Better infrastructure for cyclists (such as cycle lanes and advance stop lines at intersections), general traffic calming measures, and an increase in the number of people cycling in some key urban areas such as central London, have all helped to cut what risks there are. But, of course, the person who can do most about your safety on a bike is you.

The most important rule of riding safely is to ensure your visibility. The first thing a motorist who has knocked off a cyclist will say, reflexively but often truthfully, is that "I didn't see you." Bright clothing—such as a fluorescent waistcoat or cycling-specific gear with reflective strips—is always a good idea. More important still is to use lights at night or in low-light conditions. This, of course, is a legal requirement in any case. The flashing LED type work very well and have good battery life. Additional measures, such as spoke-mounted reflectors on wheels or reflective panels on panniers, all help. But these, valuable as they are, are essentially passive measures.

Active visibility means several things. First, it involves being confident and assertive about your road space and your right to occupy it. Of course, you should not ride in the middle of the road in a lordly and inconsiderate way, but neither should you hug the gutter. Not only is this dangerous for you—the edge of the road tends to be where the potholes and worst surfaces are, and you run the risk of clipping the kerb—but also it is a submissive posture that can actually make you less visible to drivers.

Second, use hand signals whenever necessary and, in fact, whenever possible. It is much safer for you, for example, when you have to pull out to pass a stationary bus to indicate your intention by signalling with your right hand. Any car trying to pass you and the bus will see you sooner and either move out to give you more room or delay their overtaking manoeuvre. Again, using a hand signal is way of affirming and asserting your presence. Signalling is also a courtesy to other road users that helps foster respect for cyclists.

It is worth remembering the driver's *aide-memoire* of 'mirror, signal, manoeuvre'—which, adapted for cycling, means look first before your signal. Looking generally means a check over your right shoulder for traffic immediately behind, before making a signal or any manoeuvre. You cannot assume that just because you've made a signal that any vehicle immediately behind will have seen it, or you, and will respond appropriately. Motorcyclists call the check over the right shoulder 'the lifesaver'—and rightly so. It should be an instinctive reflex for cyclists also.

Third—and perhaps the most important part of 'active visibility'—is to make eye contact with other road users whenever possible. This way, you can see whether you yourself have been seen. This check is particularly important when you are passing a car waiting to pull into your lane from a side road. Roundabouts are another important place to make eye contact, because drivers in a hurry to pull out are often looking further away for faster-moving vehicle traffic—and not for the cyclist who is practically upon them.

Given the importance of eye contact, remember that it is precisely the times when it is more difficult to establish it—that is, after dark and, worse still, when it is wet as well—that you have to be more careful. If you are not sure you have made eye contact with a driver who may move into your path, then make no assumptions about whether he has seen you. Slow down if necessary and be prepared to make an emergency stop.

The final part of being actively visible is to avoid riding into the blindspots of vehicles. Generally, car drivers in cities are better at using their side mirrors than drivers less accustomed to large numbers of cyclists and motorcyclists, but you should still take care when moving up the inside and overtaking stationary or slow-moving traffic. Even more important is never to get alongside the near side of a large truck or articulated lorry unless you can see that your way ahead is completely clear and that there is no danger that the heavy goods vehicle may be about to make a left turn. Even when their mirrors are correctly adjusted, these vehicles have a substantial blindspot behind the driver's cab on the inside (some advertise this fact on stickers). This, combined with the fact that long vehicles tend to 'cut' the corner dramatically when executing a turn, makes lorries a serious threat. Although cycling fatalities are relatively rare, the left-turning lorry is a major cause of those that do occur. Avoid the scenario entirely and you automatically make your cycling substantially safer.

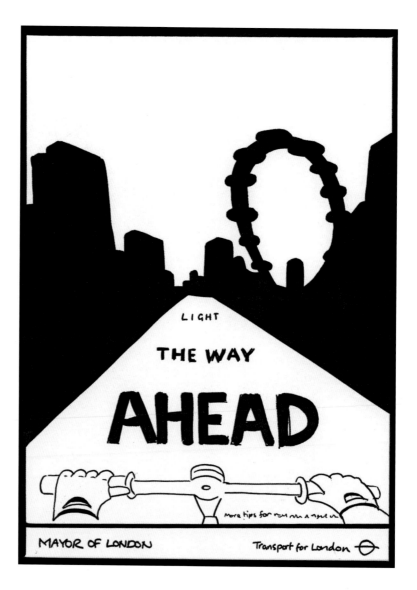

Other safe cycling measures

One thing that helps is to make reasonably brisk progress, if you can. I don't mean that you should move to a racing bike and charge around as fast as you can. Always ride at a speed appropriate to the conditions—and that can mean pretty slowly if you're having to work your way through lines of traffic. But if you can ride at a reasonable speed when the way ahead is clear, it helps in two ways—one objective, the other subjective. The objective bit is that, paradoxically perhaps, a bike is a more stable entity and is easier to control at 25 kilometres per hour than it is at five—people wobble on bikes when they are going very slowly. The subjective side is that if there is less of a differential between your speed and the speed of the ambient traffic, then you will feel safer and more 'part' of that traffic than like a minnow struggling in the wake of a passing leviathan.

Keeping your bike in a reasonable state of roadworthiness is important too. Never ride a bike that has only one brake functioning properly, for instance. Brake pads and cables especially should be checked regularly and, if necessary, changed. Often good brake operation is just a matter of adjusting cable tension. Likewise, if your gears are slipping or jumping, then it is time to take care of it or get your bike professionally serviced. Keep your tyres properly pumped up—a deflated tyre is more prone to damage and puncturing, and will have less grip in a turn.

The state of urban roads often leaves a lot to be desired. When you are riding, always try to look ahead for potential trouble. Practise avoiding potholes entirely, if possible. There is a technique for skirting round the unforeseen crater at the last minute by just moving the bike under you in a swift, twitch-like mini-swerve without substantially altering the direction of travel of your upper body. Alternatively, if a hole really cannot be avoided, try to cushion the blow by lifting your body slightly out of the saddle and moving your weight back. Try to make the front of the bike 'light' so that it doesn't crash down in to the hollow, and then use your legs as shock absorbers so that your whole weight does not bear down on the back wheel as it runs over the hole. Both of these techniques are worth experimenting with so that the habit is fairly automatic when the real thing comes along.

Take special care, when surfaces are wet, of road 'furniture' such as manhole covers, grates, storm drains and the like. Anything made of metal is likely to be very slippery when damp. The additional risk is that straight edges or ridges on the road running near-parallel to your wheels can trap your wheel and cause a 'tramlining' effect (that is, rather as if your wheel had got stuck in the recess of a tramline—self-evidently hazardous to cyclists). When this happens, the bike can go one way, while you go another. Best avoided.

Whenever possible, always give parked cars the full width of a door (approximately one metre) as you pass. This is not always possible; if not, then it's best to slow down enough to give yourself the chance of avoiding collision in case of emergency. It can help to keep an eye out for parked cars that actually have passengers sitting in them, and remember that cars parked near a row of shops are inherently more likely to have someone getting in and out. In shopping areas, it's also worth bearing in mind that occasionally passengers will get out of cars that are not pulled in to the kerb—and if you are riding past traffic on the inside, you can easily be caught out by someone opening a door on your right, rather than on your left.

Do obey traffic signals and road signs. Pay particular attention to signals giving priority to pedestrians. A plea: please do not run red lights. It can be tempting, but it's illegal and inconsiderate, and gives cyclists a bad name. It is also at your own risk—since you will always be at fault if you cause or are involved in an accident as a result of crashing a red. If you have not taken a driving test, then it is worth picking up a copy of *The Highway Code* and familiarising yourself with the rules of the road and common signage, especially those sections that particularly affect cyclists.

Until recently, cycle training courses were thin on the ground. Children might get offered a proficiency course at school, but there was very little for adults. That has now changed: increasingly, local authorities offer cycle training courses for little or no cost. More and more children are getting very well trained at school. And it is possible for adults to enrol themselves for a private course at one of the growing number of agencies and consultancies that offer cycle training. If you want to gain confidence quickly, this is a very good way to go. Courses are tailored for everyone from absolute beginners, to people who can cycle but are anxious about riding in busy traffic, to regular cyclists who want to brush up on their skills and gain confidence. Whatever level you are at, this is highly recommended. Apart from anything, it's fun!

Helmets: As discussed in the previous chapter, the contribution of helmets to cycling safety is an issue of some controversy. Let us call it a matter of individual conscience and personal preference, but certainly many people feel more secure and protected if they do wear a helmet. For what it's worth, I almost always choose to wear a helmet. If you've ever had a fall which involved writing off a helmet, you tend to have a fairly solid, albeit unscientific, sense that it saved you from a potentially much more serious injury. But there will always be the sceptics and refuseniks.

If you do wear a helmet, there are a couple of things to note. First, they do not last for ever. The expanded polystyrene of the main structure (usually with a thin plastic skin on the outside) does eventually degrade and lose its strength. You should get at least five years' life out of a helmet, but constant exposure to heat and bright sunlight can hasten the decay. Second, if you do have an accident while wearing a helmet and suspect that it sustained a blow, then you should check it very carefully for fractures and cracks. Essentially, bike helmets are good for

No cycling.

Cycle route ahead.

Route to be used by bicycles only.

Area shared by bicycles and pedestrians.

Contra-flow cycle lane.

Start of with-flow bicycle and bus lane.

With-flow bicycle lane.

one crash and one only: they are designed to absorb impacts partly by fragmenting, rather like the 'crumple zones' engineered into modern cars. If in doubt, buy a new one; a damaged one will not protect you the next time. Third, ensure that your helmet fits you well (i.e., snugly), and adjust the straps regularly to maintain a good fit and position. The correct position is one where the front of the helmet comes down low over your brow, to just above your eyebrows. If you can see your hairline (or where your hairline used to be), it means the helmet is tilted too far back; it needs to sit forward to be effective.

Road rage is an inherent risk for cyclists—usually as victims, but occasionally as perpetrators. It is inevitable that you will come across numerous examples of rude, bad and dangerous behaviour by other road users—most commonly at the hands of motorists. Tempting as it is to retaliate by shouting or screaming at the offender, getting into an argument is rarely worth it. If you ride around permanently on a short fuse, you will not find any shortage of incidents to set you off. Road rage incidents tend to leave both parties feeling self-righteously aggrieved and murderous, without resolution. Sometimes it may be impossible not to vent your frustration, but personally I find things work better if I take the karmic approach and let it ride. It is a big drain on one's emotional energy to get into fights all the time, and once the adrenalin has worn off, you usually discover that you have subtly but perceptibly stepped off the moral high ground by getting into an ugly encounter.

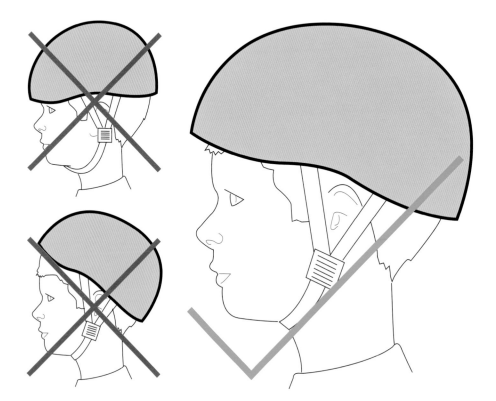

Worst case scenario

If you are involved in an accident, what should you do? First, the vast majority of incidents involving cyclists are minor and trivial. In other words, the chances are you won't hurt yourself. Or the worst you will suffer are a couple of grazes and bruises. If the accident is self-inflicted (e.g., you clip the kerb and fall off), then still give yourself time to take a proper check of your condition first, and then, once you are satisfied that your are physically all right, your bike's condition. Bear in mind that even a minor fall can leave you in mild shock, and not necessarily in a completely rational state. It might be a good idea to lock up your bike and find somewhere to sit down and perhaps have a hot drink until you feel less shaken.

If another party is involved in the incident, then you need to try to enlist the help of a witness. If you show any sign of being hurt, it is likely that someone will be volunteering to help you already. But if at all possible you need to establish if there is anyone present who saw the incident. Whatever state you're in, it is highly advisable to secure this person's agreement to provide their contact details and agree to act as a witness, if necessary. Unfortunately, it is all too common for motorists involved in a collision with a cyclist to be contrite and apologetic in the heat of the moment, only later to decide that they bore no responsibility whatsoever. An independent witness in these circumstances, who is able to verify your version of events, is absolutely essential.

If an accident has resulted in injury, it is entirely legitimate to ask a bystander to call the police. In fact, it is illegal not to report a road accident resulting in injury. A police officer will take details and statements from the parties involved and any witnesses; this may prove very important to your case at a later date, should you mount a claim for compensation.

If you have any injury, or if your bicycle has sustained any damage, then it is likely that you may be able to claim damages from the other party's insurer. Assuming the other party is a motorist, you need to obtain the driver's name, address, and insurer. Make a note also of the vehicle's registration number, its make and model. If possible, ask a witness to take a note of the same. Note the time and location of the incident. If there has been a collision, even if it does not appear to have resulted in damage or injury, still insist on this protocol. Sometimes, only later will an orthopaedic injury such as whiplash become apparent. Equally, you may not notice at first that your bike is damaged.

If you belong to an organisation such as British Cycling, the Cyclists Touring Club, or London Cycling Campaign, then your membership will provide access to legal advice and may also include third party insurance in case of a claim against you (eg, by a pedestrian). This in itself is quite sufficient a reason to belong to any of these institutions. Even if you do not, there are many legal firms specialising in personal injury claims who may be willing to take on your case on a conditional 'no win, no fee' basis. But let's hope it never happens.

Cycling safely with children

Children can learn to ride a bike unsupported by stabilisers (sometimes called training wheels) as young as four or five. Most children should be able to learn to ride a bike quickly by the age of eight or nine, but in every case it's best to let the child set the pace and not force the issue. Training wheels are usually adjustable, and one intermediate measure is to slightly raise the wheels on each side as the child gains in competence and confidence. This will leave the child doing more of the work of balancing as they ride than before—good practice for managing without stabilisers completely.

A park is the best place for learning to ride—well away from cars, and with plenty of open space. Another useful tip for teaching a child to ride a bicycle unsupported is to ride on the grass, not the pavement. This has several benefits: it's a softer surface for the odd, inevitable tumble; and it's actually easier to learn on because the mixture of compliance and resistance you get on grass has the effect of slowing down the steering responses. But, in the end, there isn't really a substitute for a certain amount of running along behind your child supporting them (best done by grasping under the saddle or holding the seatpost from behind). Good luck.

Once your child has mastered the essentials of staying upright, then you can move fairly quickly to riding on the pavement. Obviously, you need to be sure that your child can control the bike and stop when she wants. At this age, gears are fairly superfluous. In my experience, children only get interested in gears and are only able to use them competently quite a bit later—perhaps at the age of nine or ten.

Children learn a great deal of their behaviour by observation and imitation, so your example on the bike is important. Strictly speaking, adults are by law forbidden from cycling on the pavement. In practice, however, it is unlikely that you will be challenged on this score if you are accompanying young children on bikes. Many road crossings are now, in fact, designed to be 'shared use' (that is, for pedestrians and cyclists). If you ride sensibly and considerately, you are unlikely to have trouble on this score. But it is a good idea to make the transition from pavement to road with children when possible; there is no fixed age for this—it is a matter of judgment about when the child is ready for it.

Many children nowadays are offered cycle training at school. If this is possible, then it is extremely worthwhile. Children often take instruction better from teachers than their own parents, and the instructors will progress the children from practising in the playground to guided riding on the road.

For making the transition from park and pavement to the road, it is best to start on back streets where there is little or no traffic (and then go back to pavement riding when you reach main roads). It is generally easier for the adult to lead, especially when it is time to negotiate junctions, roundabouts and so on. This also allows the child or children to watch your actions and follow suit. For riding on the road, it is important that a child's bike be properly maintained and in good working order; it should also be equipped with lights and reflectors, just as an adult's bike should. Having the child ride behind also encourages the child to learn to ride close to another cyclist, which is a useful skill in itself—but be aware of the proximity and avoid making sudden changes of direction or stops.

There is no legal minimum age at which a child is allowed to cycle unaccompanied by an adult on the road. The question of when a child is ready to cycle on the road on their own is a judgment only the parent can make with the particular child in question. As a rule of thumb, it should probably not be until the child is big enough to be riding a full-sized (i.e. adult) bicycle—which is likely to be around the early teens. Naturally, it is a decision that will be largely affected by the immediate environment and traffic conditions in the area. However, once a child is on a full-sized bike, with at least 66 centimetre wheels, this is also the moment when riding on the pavement becomes a dubious activity in the eyes of the law.

Cycling with toddlers

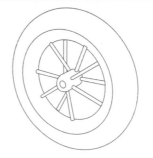

Opposite: a selection of childrens' bikes. Clockwise from top left: Islabikes Beinn 20; Islabikes Cnoc 14; Raleigh Kool; Dawes Lottie; Velowalker Velo5; Dawes Blowfish; Raleigh Molly; Raleigh GI Boys.

Below: three different ways of carrying a toddler on a bike—a toddlers seat which is affixed to the back-rack, a trailer pulled behind, and a children's extension.

Children too young to ride can be carried on bikes. The bike seats that are mounted on a rear rack above the back wheel are very secure and sturdy. Children tend to enjoy the experience of being passengers on a bike, and are largely sheltered from the elements in this position. They should, however, always wear a helmet. The seat itself should be fitted professionally by a bike shop, or by you, but only if you are confident of doing a secure job. Most important is that you should be prepared for the extra weight on the bike. Once you are riding, the child's weight is negligible compared with your own, but before you mount the bike, the top-heavy mass of a kid in the child-seat takes a bit of getting used to.

A confident toddler can easily graduate from being carried in a seat behind to a system where a seat is mounted on the top tube in front of your saddle, with struts bolted onto the down tube as foot-rests. The child simply holds onto the handlebars, and in effect rides the bike with you. It sounds intrinsically less safe than the child-seat arrangement, but is more secure than you might think. For the child who has outgrown the being passively carried stage, it is a good solution before they are ready to ride their own bike. A helmet, again, is a must for the child, whatever you do for yourself.

A further alternative, especially for families with two small children, is the trailer type of child carrier. Some parents may have instinctive misgivings about these pieces of apparatus: they seem low to the ground and vulnerable, but in practice they are highly visible and will be given a wide berth by motorists. Depending on the type of journey involved, they can be a useful solution, although they will always appeal to the already dedicated cyclist-parent. Because of the extra width involved, extra care must be taken when manoeuvring around corners. If used after dark, remember that trailers must be fully advertised with their own rear-facing red light or lights.

Another solution is the children's extension—an attachment that can be hitched to an adult's bike behind the saddle or seatpost that has a frame and rear wheel, with saddle, pedals and handlebar for the child. This, in effect, turns the adult's bike into a kind of articulated tandem. The beauty of these devices is that it is easily detachable, so can be left, for example, locked up independently at your child's school. The child can choose to pedal, if she wants, but can just coast behind her mum or dad. Being only as wide as the rest of the bicycle, it is less cumbersome and easier to ride through traffic than, say, a two-wheel trailer.

Choosing to ride

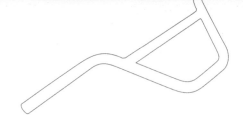

Opposite: a bike rests against a wall in Beijing. Photograph by Alistair Humphries.

No one can decide for you whether riding a bike is the best option; it is something you should discover for yourself. However, I can say that there are many good reasons to cycle. Not only is it good for you both mentally and physically, but it's also fun, efficient and available to all. Whilst you may sometimes feel more vulnerable on a bicycle than you would in a car, it is important to remember the level of control you have when cycling, and there is a great deal you can do to make yourself safe on a bike.

When you are making your decision, pause to look around you. Explore the cycle routes you could use; get a map. Notice how many lanes, advance stop lines, marked routes, and general signage there is for cyclists. See how many other cyclists there are around: the more, the better—cyclists gain safety in numbers, largely because other road users are more aware of them and make appropriate allowances for their presence. By cycling, you are contributing to the common good in numerous ways, not least because you're making it safer and more pleasant for other people to cycle just by doing it yourself.

Best of all, you discover a new type of ownership of your hometown. You gain an understanding of its topography, how its localities relate to one another. You develop a new sensibility for its character, its idiosyncrasies and secrets. When you ride your bike about town, you see it all in a new light.

You couldn't buy that experience, but in fact you get it for free. All you need to do is ride a bike. It's really that simple.

ME AND MY BIKE

My friend was paid £200 for his socks by a foot fetishist, and that's just the tip of the iceberg.

Dan Simon/UK

When Dan Simon's friend decided to become a woman, Dan decided to drive a rickshaw. It just seemed petty not to. Dan had been working the night shifts at lastminute.com, and was absolutely, officially sick to the back teeth of the world of IT. Sitting in Caffé Nero in Soho with an ex-girlfriend, he was going through everything that was wrong with his life, when an old friend, George cycled past on a rickshaw. Dan hadn't seen George for over six months, so was surprised to see that his friend appeared to have developed breasts and had changed his name to Sarah. Faced with this momentous decision, Dan had something of an epiphany: "It was then that it clicked that something was not happening in my life." He gave up his job, and after a "year of hell", plucked up the courage to approach Bug a Bugs, at the time the leading rickshaw company in London. After brief, but rigorous theoretical and practical tests, he was taken on and began his new life as a rickshaw rider.

The world of rickshaws cyclists is a friendly one. The job attracts people from a broad range of nationalities and backgrounds. It's flexible and low-commitment. Like taxis, the riders register with a company and then rent out the rickshaws (at around £85 per week or £30 per day–$150 and $55 respectively). The fares that they earn are then theirs to keep. When Dan started, there were only a handful of companies operating, and only 40 odd drivers–few enough to recognise all of them. These days the market is pretty saturated. With over 300 riders, it's impossible to keep track of them all. Nonetheless, the sense of fraternity remains, and for the most part, there is an amicable respect between rickshaw drivers–as long as they respect the highway code.

The first month of rickshaw driving is excruciating, as your muscles get used to the strain. But now Dan can comfortably work four nights a week without thinking too much of it. Rickshaws are surprisingly maneuverable. They can turn 180 degrees on the spot and are narrow enough to glide comfortably through traffic. In New York for example, rickshaws are particularly popular in peak hours and are often the transport of choice for businessmen, being much more reliable than taxis. In London, rickshaws fill a different role. Various experiments with rickshaws in the City, the financial district of London, failed, and the business is now entirely concentrated in the West End, primarily taking people from one venue to another. The average journey distance of a fare is about half a mile, usually centred around the Covent Garden and Soho areas with the odd fare further out to Notting Hill or Pimlico.

Working in the heart of London's nightlife, rickshaw drivers inevitably get their fair share of drunk people, and tend to have a whole slew of stories to tell about passengers that were encountered and propositions that were made. Dan tells of the time he took Madonna to a shoot, and of the countless pick-up lines he has had to endure. A close colleague of his was paid £200 for his socks by a foot fetishist–and that's just the tip of the iceberg.

Although it seems like a tourist attraction, most of the passengers Dan picks up are Londoners. It's surprisingly pleasant to ride in a rickshaw. The speed of travel means you can really observe the world around you, and by being partially outside you can experience the buzz of the city. In the summer the wind blows in your face and in winter you can snuggle down in the duvet provided by the driver, and it's all very romantic.

Dan doesn't intend to rickshaw forever, but as far as he's concerned, it certainly beats IT.

ME AND MY BIKE

Bikes are a great tool to get the attention of bored teens and pre-teens, because they give a young person so much freedom.

Andy Dyson/USA

Below left: Andy and his team do a safety check in a school yard.

Below right: Andy with his bike on the streets of Philadelphia.

Philadelphia is a tough city. Every year an average of 300 people are murdered, and the sound of gunshots in the street is something people in certain neighbourhoods now take in their stride. In all, it's a pretty hard place to grow up in, and a worrying amount of bored, underprivileged teenagers end up with little access to local resources, poor prospects for employment, and not much to do but get into trouble.

Andy Dyson works for a non-profit organisation called Neighbourhood Bike Works, or NBW. It was set up in 1996 in emulation of similar programmes that were instituted in Boston and New York, and its aim is to increase opportunities for youth through bicycling. One of the primary ways in which this is done is through 'Earn-a-Bike' classes, in which young people recondition bikes which have either been sent to landfill, or donated. After fulfilling certain criteria, the students earn the bike that they have done up. In Andy's words, "bikes are a great tool to get the attention of bored teens and pre-teens because they give so much freedom to a young person with no other way to get around". NBW also arranges cycle rides for youths, produces bike related art and offers job training, education in health, safety and the environment, and employment opportunities (as well as community service opportunities) for young people at risk.

Above left: Andy at the drop-in centre.

Above right: Neighbourhood Bike Works'
40th Street bike shop.

The organisation is open to all youth aged eight to 17. 95 per cent of
the kids that attend are African American, and 80 per cent are boys, with
most coming from the low-income area of West Philadelphia. Last year
around 120 new students went through the Earn-a-Bike Programme, 200
attended a seven week course, and about 600 attended workshops in
schools or community groups. 250 bikes were earned by youths or sold
by them to raise money for themselves and for the organisation. In a
medium sized city, this is no bad result. Andy puts this success down to the
expertise of the management team. NBW is run by a group of volunteers
who report to a board of trustees with a broad spectrum of backgrounds
and experience; city politics, academia, the bicycle advocacy world, bike
police, the environmental movement and people in the population that
the programme serves. Andy believes that if the scheme is to be replicated
elsewhere, this diversity of input is essential.

NBW is part of the local bicycle advocacy organisation, and as such
has been involved in numerous campaigns for cyclists' rights. It has made
a siginficant impact to the way cyclists and cycling have been treated by
motorists and by the authorities in Philadelphia. Andy believes that this is
indicative of the changing way that cyclists are perceived throughout the
United States:

Rising fuel prices mean that bicycle use is poised to make a
great leap in the US, especially in urban areas. Three hundred
thousand cars were destroyed by Hurricane Katrina and
Americans responded with their usual resourcefulness and...
rode bikes! I think that Lance Armstrong has made cycling more
respectable here, but I think that expensive gasoline will do more.

ME AND MY BIKE

I thought why am I here...
I could do this quicker
on my bike.

Tom Lynch/UK

Below: Tom Lynch in his BMX racing days.

To say that Tom Lynch likes bikes would probably be considered a gross understatement. Tom Lynch loves bikes. From his first Raleigh Chipper when he was a young lad in 1975, the bike bug had bitten him good. In 1980, a few years before the BMX boom really took off, Tom Lynch was already on one, copying the motocross moves he had seen on the telly, launching himself off every edge, ledge and ramp in the vicinity of his home.

When his father, a semi-professional boxer, noticed his son's enthusiasm he devised a training programme and started to coach him. By the time Tom was 12, he was getting up at five am, and racing for two hours before school started; by the time he was 14 he was competing in the World Championships; and by the time he was 16, he had already won the regional, national and European Championships, and had been moved into Superclass division. His career as a BMX champ lasted almost 20 years, over which period he accumulated over 500 trophies and prizes. By the time he hit his mid thirties, however, he could feel himself slowing down, and in 1994, he had to recognise that his racing career was over.

Ever since an accident in his youth, when he had to be taken from school in an ambulance, Tom had been drawn to the caring profession, and so, after a few years working as coach, Tom found his second calling as a paramedic with the ambulance service.

It was in 1998, sitting in the back of the ambulance on a call-out in central London, stuck in traffic, that Tom had his revelation: "I thought 'why am I here? I'm just here because the traffic's holding us back. I could do this quicker on my bike.'"

Below left: The array of equipment that
each cycle-ambulance is kitted out with.

Below right: Tom Lynch on a call out.

With the same relentless drive that had taken him to the BMX championships, Tom began to pursue his vision. By 2000, he had been given the go-ahead to launch a cycle-response trial. Working alone, he was dispatched on his bike to call outs within a five-mile radius, and to his delight, found that he was beating the ambulances 88 per cent of the time. The trial was deemed a success and London Ambulance's Cycle Response Unit (CRU) was officially instated.

Modelled on the International Police Mountain Bike Association, Tom set up a cycle training scheme for paramedics, instituting physical fitness and safely tests, and drawing on his own experience to coach the participants. Today there are 16 cyclists working for CRU. Working in the same five-mile radius that Tom initially scouted out, they respond to a range of calls—usually of lower-priority, but sometimes more serious incidents. Dashing out on their Specialized Rockhoppers, their response time average is a mere six minutes, and they have frequently been known to arrive on scene whilst the caller is still on the phone. Equipped with a 20 kilogram pack of medical supplies (including a mini set of defibrillators and a mini oxygen tank), they assess the situation, provide immediate assistance, and if transport and hospital admittance is required, arrange for an ambulance.

Since their establishment, there has been a 50 per cent reduction in ambulance cancellations; the team saves £80,000 ($140,000) in vehicle non-dispatch costs, £2,000 ($3,500) in fuel and 251 hours of ambulance availability.

With their distinctive uniforms and bicycles, bicycle ambulances have become a common sight in Central London, and Tom has received numerous awards for his commitment and dedication to the scheme. Other UK cities such as Norwich, Plymouth and Nottingham, as well as other emergency response services, are hoping to introduce similar units in the near future.

ME AND MY BIKE

Cycling is going to grow over the next decade quite spectacularly.... The South East is approaching gridlock!

Nick Harvey/UK

Nick Harvey is the coordinator of National Bike Week, the UK's only annual celebration of cycling. In the late 1970s Nick joined a PR consultancy who did some work for a cycle manufacturer, and in his own words, has "never lost enthusiasm for promoting cycling". A keen cyclist, Nick owns 12 bikes, including a mountain bike for off-road cycling, a racing bike for keeping fit and a modern Penny Farthing, which he finds quite tricky to ride. He commutes to work on the train and on his fold-up Brompton bike.

Established in 1923 by the Cyclists' Touring Club (CTC), Bike Week has been held almost every year, but in the past seven years it has grown in size dramatically, with a lottery grant for the Millennium Celebration of Cycling ensuring that this century's cycling started with a bang. In 2001, however, Bike Week faced difficulties as Foot and Mouth Disease spread across England, and there were fears at the beginning of the year that cycling in rural areas could help to spread the disease. However, as the danger subsided, the government asked Nick to promote a return to the countryside by cyclists in the spring, and he managed to co-ordinate a national Bike Week in only ten weeks.

Since then, Bike Week has got bigger and better, and this year Nick expects there will be 1,500 events held around the country, with over 225,000 participants. There is always a London to Brighton bike ride which attracts in excess of 27,000 people, and the Cyclist Touring Club hold a cycle show and rally in York. Individual cycling enthusiasts and promoters also organise their own public events, which all aim to get more people cycling more often. Part of Bike Week is a 'Bike2Work' promotion, where commuters are encouraged to cycle rather than drive. There is also a 'Bike2School week' earlier in the year, intended to encourage school children to take part in National Standard cycling lessons and get on their bikes. In Nick's words:

> 50 per cent of journeys made by car are under five miles—a distance which can easily be cycled. We want to encourage the high number of drivers who travel short distances in cars to travel by bike. There are environmental benefits, fitness benefits, cost benefits- and in urban areas, you often get to work quicker.

Nick is positive about the future of cycling in England:

> I think cycling is going to grow over the next decade quite spectacularly. The number of cyclists in London has doubled over the past five years, due not only to the congestion charge, but also to good maps and infrastructure improvements. There are cycle lanes, and cyclists can go the wrong way down many one way streets now. London's example will encourage others. In many urban areas, they will have no choice—traffic is a nightmare. The South East is approaching gridlock!

Bike Week therefore encourages people to do both themselves and the environment a favour—to get cycling more often.

Cycle sport

Road racing

Opposite: mountain bikers cycle the Fruita Trail. Photograph by Dean Taylor.

Below: the Tour of Britain is a blue ribband event that is run every year in the UK at the end of August.

Road racing is the dominant discipline in cycle sport, the area where most of money and prestige is to be found. The professional racing season is divided into two different types of event–stage races and one-day 'grands prix'. A stage race is run over anything from three days to three weeks, where the overall result is based on the best aggregate time favouring the consistent all-rounder. Of the stage races, there are three grand tours–the Giro d'Italia , the Vuelta d'Espana, and most famous of all, the blue ribband event, the Tour de France.

Many of the best-known one-day races form the highlights of the early part of the season, the 'spring classics' such as the Milan-San Remo, the Tour of Flanders and the 'queen of the classics' itself, the Paris-Roubaix. Like the Tour de France, many of these races date from the very origins of cycle sport at the end of the nineteenth and beginning of the twentieth centuries. With courses often in excess of 250 kilometres, they are formidable tests of endurance and tactical nous—only the strongest on the day, psychologically as well as physically, will prevail. The courses do not cover mountainous areas, as the grand tours do—most are based in the relatively flat lands of Belgium and northern France. But in the case of the Tour of Flanders, for example, the short, steep cobbled climbs known as 'murs', often serve to provide the decisive moment in the race in the final kilometres.

In the case of the Paris-Roubaix, the parcours (the 'course') includes numerous sections of ancient cobbled farm tracks—at best, dusty in the dry, but in the wet, muddy and treacherously slippery—which cause the key splits and selections of the main group in the race. The race passes through a bleak landscape of agricultural land and former mining communities, and often the racers arrive at the velodrome in Roubaix for a finale lap so covered in grime that they almost resemble miners after a shift down the pit. Appropriately enough, to the victor in this ultimate 'hard man's' race gets not a traditional gilded cup, but a heavy lump of granite—one of the blocks of pavé that make the race what it is.

The spring classics are far from the only one day events, and the professional season traditionally culminates with other great races saturated in tradition such as the Tour of Lombardy, known as the 'ride of the falling leaves'. The World Championship road race also comes towards the end of the season—its winner is entitled to wear the coveted rainbow-striped jersey for the following year. Some of these events move in and out of favour over time. In recent years, for example, the 'Worlds' have not been contested by some of the biggest names in cycling because they have been held so late in the year (October) that many have already ended their season. But the landmarks endure, each with their own mythology and their legendary heroes among the roster of past winners.

The peloton, 'drafting' and tactics

The bunch or pack, which constitutes the main field of riders in all these races, is often referred to by commentators as the 'peloton'. The French word means literally 'a ball', and when you watch an aerial view of the Tour de France from one of the helicopter-mounted cameras, you begin to see the figurative truth of the description: the way the peloton elongates and then reforms in tight group, as the riders speed up and slow down has an organic quality that is rather like a ball of dough or putty being stretched out and then rolled back up.

A smaller group that detaches itself from the peloton is known as a 'breakaway' or a 'break'. A crucial factor in road racing is wind resistance. Most of the work that a cyclist has to do to maintain a racing speed is forcing his way through the wall of air confronting him. The rider directly behind him is doing about a third less work, and the rider behind him only about half the work of the first rider. In other words, slipstreaming makes a huge difference. But to gain the advantage of hiding from the wind by ducking into the hole made by the cyclist in front, you have to ride close together—your front wheel perhaps just 20-30 centimetres from the rear wheel of the rider ahead of you. This is why racers stick so close together in the peloton. If you watch a bike race on television carefully you can sometimes make out that, while the riders at the front are pedalling hard, the riders in the middle of the bunch are scarcely pedalling at all—the 'drafting' effect is so powerful that they are almost being sucked along. It is on this basic principle that the entire tactical game of road racing is based.

Of course, the way racers ride so close together is an accident waiting to happen. Although these professionals are extremely skilled bike handlers who spend hundreds of hours and thousands of kilometres in the saddle every year, crashes are a common occurrence—especially, although it might seem paradoxical, on the flat stages that generally mark the beginning of the big stage races like the Tour de France. These crashes—or *chutes*, as the French call them—are partly caused by the sheer speed of these stages, partly by the slightly more reckless competitiveness and keenness of the rider, and but partly because such stages are often affected by cross-winds, which make the whole business of 'drafting' more

Above left: the Belgian racer, Romain Maes with Gabriel Ruozzi taking a moment to chat at the start of a stage in the 1935 Tour de France.

Above right: Ainslie Baumann wins a stage at the Tour of Britain.

complex and demanding. In a large peloton (the Tour de France starts with 198 riders), there is also a concertina effect: it only takes the riders at the front to relax their pace a little for the riders at the back to suddenly find themselves riding into the back of riders in front. For this reason, potential winners of the Tour always try to ride relatively close to the front of the peloton. They might have to do more work to stay there, but it's safer. For the guys who ride towards the back of the peloton, it's a trade-off: they are reserving their energy, but they're also taking a bigger risk of being involved in a crash.

The principle of drafting also underlies what happens when a group of riders goes on the attack. In any race, there will always be a series of attacks. One rider will sprint ahead of the peloton and hope to be joined by others. If he is lucky, a small group of anything from two or three up to fifteen or twenty riders will join him. For an attack to be effective, they have to keep their speed higher than the main bunch. The only way they can achieve is this is by co-operation, taking turns to set the pace in a highly organised way, each coming to the front for a 'pull' into the wind. Often, if the attack group is too large, the co-operation tends to break down: it is too easy for some riders to 'hide' and not take their turn, or some riders may be under team orders just to 'police' the break but not contribute to its success.

The paradox of this co-operation, of course, is that it involves competitors on different teams coming together in mutual aid. But such alliances can only be temporary. Always, towards the end of a stage, where a break has successfully prised an advantage of several minutes over the peloton, you will see the co-operation break down and breakaway riders starting to attack each other to try to secure the individual win; or they stop working together to save some strength for the final dash. If the break's advantage over the fast-moving peloton is only a few seconds, then they risk getting caught and swept up in the bunch before the finish line. That is their gamble. So the closing kilometres of a stage or a one-day race often see a nail-baiting finale involving not only a trial of strength but also a severe test of nerve.

How the teams work

What may also seem rather mystifying to begin with is that professional cycling is both a team sport and an individual competition. Above all, it is the sole winner who is feted, and if you do not make it onto the podium (that is, by being in the top three finishers), no one really notices or cares where you came. And yet, every event is contested by ten or a dozen teams, so how does this work—and what decides who emerges as the winner?

The simple answer is that teams almost always operate with a 'team leader'—the rider designated as the team's best, the one most likely to succeed in any given race. Occasionally, where there is not a clear candidate for the role, or where the team has such strength in depth that more than one member can reasonably stake a claim to be a possible winner, teams have more than one leader. But this is often a risky strategy, liable to create tension and strife within the team.

Above: handcycling, which provides a cycling alternative for wheelchair users, and for people with and without disabilities, is growing in popularity and was introduced to the Athens Paralympics in 2004.

The identity of a given team leader will vary from event to event. A team's favourite for the Tour de France is unlikely to be the same rider who is considered to have a shot at carrying off the cobble in the Paris-Roubaix. For one thing, riders have to manage their 'form' and try to hit their peak at the right time for a given event. In the old days (up until the late 1970s), it was not unusual for all the big names to compete in all the major events, including all three grand tours. Since the 1980s it has become increasingly the trend for the world's best to focus on a few specific goals—chiefly on capturing the Tour de France, the biggest prize of them all and one of the largest sporting events in the world. By the time Lance Armstrong, seven times winner of the Tour, came into his own, this strategy had reached its apogee: the Tour was the season's sole objective for him. Results in other races were irrelevant; they were merely for training and preparation. This means, for instance, that comparisons between Lance, dominant cyclist of the past decade, and Eddy Merckx, the most prolific winner of the 1970s, are virtually impossible to draw.

A good leader will be able to rely on considerable practical and tactical help from team members. This can be as humdrum as junior members of the squad falling behind the peloton, in order to pick up extra supplies of food and drink for the rest of the team—hence the nicknames for such riders, 'domestiques', literally servants, or 'bottle-carriers'. But just as often it can involve team members forming a protective cordon around their team leader at stressful moments in a race (such as the final kilometres of an early, flat, 'sprinters' stage of the Tour).

In stage races, the role of the directeur sportif (team manager or 'DS') is crucial. In modern bike races, the DS is in contact with his team members via a radio link, and can give tactical instructions in real time as the day's racing develops. The DS usually rides in a team car behind the peloton, but if the race splits into several groups (as it always does in the high mountains, for instance), the team cars will be permitted to move forward in front of some groups in order to support their rider or riders at the front of the race.

The team car carries a mechanic as well as the DS and will be loaded with spare bikes and wheels, drink, food, clothing and so on. There will also generally be neutral service vehicles in major races, and then there will be race officials—the *commissaire* and his assistants—in their cars, and members of the press behind them. Not to mention the big motorbikes with pillion-passenger photographers and TV cameramen aboard. All in all, major professional races travel with a considerable convoy of vehicles.

Below: Romain Maes at the start of the 1935 Tour de France, which he went on to lead from start to finish.

Often, you will see one particular team doing all the pace-setting work at the front of the peloton. This may be because they are chasing a breakaway group which threatens to challenge their leader's advantage; or it may simply be that they are setting a fast pace in order to discourage such an attack. Sometimes, teams cooperate, either informally or by prior agreement, when their respective interests coincide. On a 'sprinters' stage, for example, it is common to see several teams vying for places at the head of affairs in the closing kilometres because each will have its sprint specialist whom they are trying to manoeuvre into the perfect position for the final, explosive burst in the last 200–300 metres. Sprinters tend to be larger, heavier riders, with muscles that have a high proportion of fast-twitch fibres (compared with the slow-twitch fibres that do the majority of work in aerobic endurance events); they can produce phenomenal amounts of power for short periods. It is common for speeds of 60–70 kilometres per hour to be reached in these final seconds of stages.

Besides the leader and a sprint specialist, a team will have one or two specialist climbers to help the team leader in the mountains or possibly to win mountain stages individually. There may also be a specialist time triallist for the stages that are individual races against the clock. And then there will be several all-rounders, who may be good enough to win stages if they get in the right moves, but will otherwise work as domestiques for the team leader. In professional bike racing, teams are looking not only at the overall result, but at achieving intermediate goals such as stage victories or wins in some of the minor competitions (in the Tour de France, for example, the green and polka dot jerseys for most consistent finisher and best climber respectively). Many teams will not have a realistic chance of getting their team leader on the podium, so stage wins become a vital way of the team winning the favourable publicity sponsors expect.

Above: Jan Ullrich and Andreas Kloeden
cycling for the German T-Mobile team.

During a long stage, of perhaps 250 kilometres or more, there may appear to be lulls and longeurs, but for most riders these are likely to be momentary only. They are almost constantly having to think and work. Sometimes, this may be as simple as forming a mini-peloton of team-mates around their team leader, to protect him and ensure that he is not isolated should any mishap befall. If he punctures, for example, a team- mate may well give his leader one of his good wheels and then wait for a replacement from the team car soon afterwards–just so that the leader does not lose his position in the race or have to exert himself more than necessary. Sacrifice is the rule for the domestique; it is how he pays his dues and earns his wages. By custom, the team's winnings are shared equally among all its members. The cheque for winning the Tour de France does not go to the man on the podium alone, but is divided (at least) nine ways among his team-mates who have helped him, day after day, to get there.

On other occasions, a team will have to be more active at the front of the bunch. If an attack has occurred that contains a rider who is highly enough placed overall to threaten their team leader's position in the general classification (the 'GC') all the team members will make their way to the front of the peloton to lend their strength to chasing the group in front. Alternatively, a team may have a plan, having studied the 'parcours' (the course) that involves trying to control the race and place their specialist sprinter in the best possible position to win the stage. In that case, the team will try to ride at the front for the last hour or so of the race setting a high pace to discourage other attacks and to create a launch pad for their sprinter. In reality, there will often be two or three other teams with exactly the same idea; the idea of 'controlling the race' in this context becomes optimistic, to say the least. A team may try to impose itself, but with so many other riders all keen to get in on the act, it is unlikely that one team will be strong enough to have it all its own way. The final kilometres of the opening, usually flat stages of the Tour de France (and other stage races) thus become a ferocious dogfight, with much jockeying for position and big risks being taken—sometimes riders lean on one another or push to stay well-placed for the sprint. Contact is legal if it's within reason and is not adjudged by the race commissaire and his officials to constitute dangerous or reckless riding.

In the later, mountainous stages of the race, the rigours of climbs which go on for ten, 20, or even 30 kilometres, partly eliminate the possibility of team tactics—the world's best climbers are a self-selecting elite. Even here, though, a team leader will usually have one team-mate who is a specialist climber to act as his loyal lieutenant in the mountains— setting a tough tempo, chasing down attackers, and so on. In this way, a DS will aim to recruit a wide range of rider types, with a variety and balance of talents and specialisms.

The team leader must be the ultimate all-rounder. A rider who (ideally) never has an 'off day', who can climb with the best of the specialist climbers, but who is also in the top ten, or better, top three, time triallists (that is, in the individual race against the clock, which generally account for two or three stages of the Tour), and who has the mental and psychological strength to dominate a race. Pure climbers are, by definition, not the best time triallists. They have a great power-to-weight ratio, and superb aerobic capacity, but time trialling is a discipline that requires sustained power, in terms of absolute numbers of wattage output. A climber will often be small—in the 60-65 kilogram range. Good time triallists are intrinsically more powerful riders. The all-rounder is an ideal blend of power-to-weight, aerobic capacity, pure power and pure speed—in many ways, the number of riders who have the potential to be a Tour de France winner, or even a leader is severely limited by genetic factors. Lung capacity, aerobic fitness potential, and the ability to train hard, recover and benefit, are to a great extent congenital gifts.

Armstrong was the strongest cyclist of his generation, possibly the best of all time, but he also led the way in redefining the meaning of team leader. Armstrong's squads were extremely disciplined: no internal challenger to the American's status was tolerated, no personal agendas or individual goals were allowed to get in the way of the overall strategy of putting Armstrong in the yellow jersey and first spot on the winner's podium. Few other teams could match this discipline and focus, and many of his potential challengers were hamstrung by half-hearted team support or ambiguity about who the leader really was.

Below: the cover of the 1978
Raleigh catalogue.

Some of the bigger, more richly-sponsored squads will have teams competing at different concurrent events. Each rider's season will be planned out in advance, with particular targets in mind, so that he arrives at the key competitions on best possible form. A pro cyclist's training is organised around the concept of 'periodisation'. Having good form means living on a knife edge. Top athletes, like professional cyclists, are so highly trained and conditioned that they are often in danger of suppressing their immune systems with the demands they place on their bodies, making them vulnerable to colds and other viral infections. Pro cyclists often take extra precautions to avoid crowded public places and take special care with personal hygiene (one I read about even avoids pressing the buttons in hotel lifts because of fears of picking up a bug). Periodisation means managing an athlete's training and racing schedule so that he has made the maximum possible adjustment to the physiological stimulus of hard exercise, and then 'tapering' down the training effort as the key event draws near—so that the athlete arrives at it both rested and at peak fitness.

RIDE WITH THE WINNER.
TEAM RALEIGH

Raleigh bicycles. Rampar bicycles. Parts and accessories.

A day in the life of a pro

The professional cyclist's typical day during a stage race will begin with an early start, waking in a hotel at perhaps seven o'clock for a big breakfast with the rest of the team—muesli, fruit, eggs, rolls, juice, coffee, cakes, even pasta. On a long stage, riders can easily burn 7,000-8,000 calories— approximately four times what a sedentary person would need per day to maintain their weight. Although cyclists are provided with packed lunches supplied out on the road by team assistants handing up *musettes*, or bags, at designated feeding stations en route, it can actually be difficult for them to get enough calories every day. It is common for riders to lose several kilograms in the course of a three-week stage race—and these are guys who already have body-fat percentages in the low single figures to start with (a normal, healthy male will have a body-fat percentage of around 15 per cent; women's different physiology means they tend to have a slightly higher percentage, 15-20 per cent).

As great a risk as not getting enough calories is dehydration. Dehydration causes a rapid and potentially catastrophic loss of performance. Riders sometimes talk about getting 'the knock' or 'the bonk', or 'hitting the wall', or 'blowing up'—all expressions describing the sudden onset of fatigue in a race. Sometimes this can be due to plain exhaustion, but it is much more likely that the problem is either dehydration or the fact that the muscles have simply run out of fuel because the rider has not eaten enough to replace the energy he has used. Dehydration usually sets in more quickly than the 'hunger knock', even though the effects may feel and seem quite similar to the rider. It is very common for racers to consume an 'isotonic' energy drink to combat both problems. This will be mainly water, but with a powdered carbohydrate mix added, often also containing salts and trace minerals so that it includes electrolytes than enable swifter absorption by the stomach than could occur with plain water. In hot weather (in southern Europe), each rider will need to consume as much as four to five litres, or even more, during the course of a race, so it is a common spectacle to see domestiques dispatched back to the team car to fetch extra bottles, which they stuff up their jerseys until they rejoin the main bunch where they can distribute the bottles to team-mates—hence their alternative nickname 'water carrier'.

After breakfast, there will generally be a team meeting called by the directeur sportif, in which he will run through the profile of that day's stage (its distance and the terrain, where the feeding stations will be, where the likely places for attacks by other teams might occur, and so on). He will also discuss the strategy for the day—to attack, or to defend, or to save energy for future stages—and to give specific tactical instructions. For example, there will often be a rider on the team who will not be a challenger for the overall result in the GC, but who will be singled out as capable of winning a single stage.

The meeting over, the riders go to change into their racing gear
(lycra shorts, polyamide jerseys, mitts and helmet, all bearing the team
sponsors' logos), prepare themselves and collect their bikes from the team
mechanic. They are then obliged to 'sign on' a register of all the riders
before they can start the stage. A rider who is ill or injured will not sign on,
and is therefore eliminated (or disqualified); he may not restart the race at
a later stage.

For four, five or six hours, the riders do their job. There's rarely such
a thing as an easy day in the saddle for a professional cyclist. They toil,
they sweat, and they suffer. For a chosen few, there will be the consolation
of seeing their photo in *L'Equipe* and the other sports papers the next
morning—a stage win, perhaps, the presentation of the leader's jersey, or
the coronation of the king of the mountains winner. But for most, it is just
another day at the office.

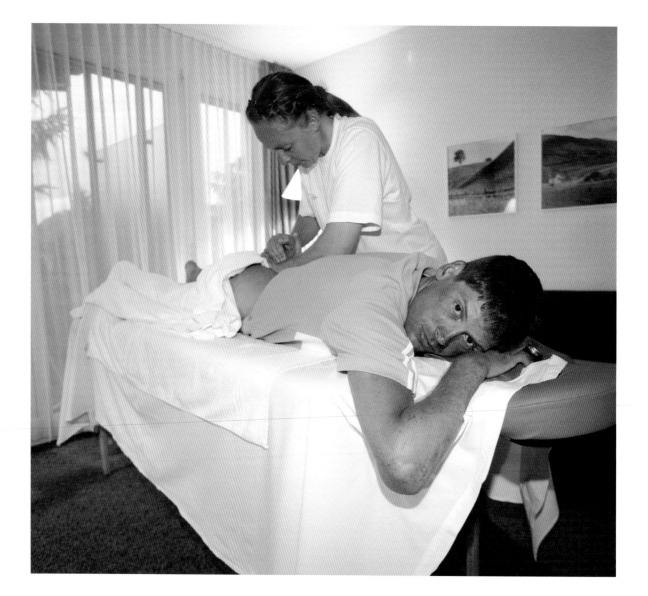

After a race, or stage, is over, the team will regroup at the team bus. A mechanic will take their bikes to be cleaned and serviced overnight, ready for the next day's racing. The riders themselves can clean up and relax on the bus on the way back to the hotel. The first thing they will do is drink a high-carbohydrate and protein energy beverage, and start snacking. After intense exercise, there is a narrow window of only an hour or so during which the body can most efficiently replenish its energy stores. The riders' recovery depends on making the most of that opportunity. Back at the hotel, the riders will shower and change, and then take a visit from the team's *soigneur* (or *soigneuse*, literally 'carer'). The *soigneur's* job is to take care of the riders' needs and comforts, from packing their favourite foods in the *musettes*, to meticulously washing all the drinking bottles and doing the daily laundry of shorts, jerseys, socks and mitts. But the traditional and perhaps most important job of the soigneur is to provide a post-ride massage. This is one of the rituals of professional cycle racing, the idea that the toxins developed by the over-stressed leg muscles can be eased away by a deep massage. Sometimes pros will even give interviews to journalists as they are getting their massage, covered only in a towel, their shaved legs a deep mahogany below where their cycle shorts end but anemic white above.

Why do racing cyclists shave their legs? Partly because the process of cleansing and massage is much easier if they are shaved. Partly also because, supposedly, it is easier to treat the grazes that occur as a result of a crash if the surface of the skin is smooth. Partly, perhaps, because it is believed that shaved legs contribute to aerodynamic efficiency and make the cyclist faster. But most of all, they do it because everyone else does and so it is simply what looks right. Cycle racing is a sport which has a highly developed sense of its own aesthetic.

While the riders' legs are being attended to, the team mechanic will be busy washing, cleaning, repairing and preparing their bikes for the next day's stage. Tyres will be changed regularly, chains almost daily; everything must work perfectly and as new. Sometimes the team bus will have to drive through the night to reach the next day's departure point in the case of a transfer between stages. The rest of the team will probably catch a flight if the distance is substantial.

After their massage, the team will gather for supper. A professional squad may even have its own chef to prepare the riders' favourite meals. Once again, a large number of calories is consumed, and there is quality as well as quantity—riders will eat plenty of salad, vegetables and fresh fruit. Water is on the table, but wine rarely—perhaps a token glass of champagne will be taken if the team has something to celebrate, a stage win or a rider's birthday, but abstinence is the rule. Alcohol places additional demands on the metabolism, interfering with liver function and therefore the body's ability to store fuel (since the liver is the primary source of energy after what is retained in the muscles is used). The DS may use the opportunity to debrief on the day's events, discuss how the tactical plan unfolded, what worked and what didn't. After dinner, riders return to their rooms, to relax, unwind, watch TV, read, call their loved ones... but soon to sleep. In a stage race, ability to recover is vital; with the extraordinary demands placed by six or seven hours in the saddle, professional cyclists often need to sleep more than average–nine or ten hours a night is normal. To be ready for the next day's relentless slog.

All professional sports require exceptional levels of focus and dedication, but the cyclist's requires a special degree of sacrifice and endurance. At least, in the modern era, it is a fairly well rewarded sport at the top level–not on a par with professional football, perhaps, but a good living all the same. In bygone days, pros worked like dogs, many to escape what would otherwise have been a life of back-breaking fieldwork in agriculture, but they often reached the ends of their careers with little to show for it. Traditionally, they might take their modest savings and open a bike shop, capitalising on their limited fame among the cycling fraternity, or perhaps a bar. After their hard life on the road, many did not take great care of themselves in retirement. That and, in some cases perhaps, the long-term effect of years of using illegal drugs such as amphetamines, took their toll: the life expectancy of a professional cyclist was, at least until relatively recently, in the early fifties.

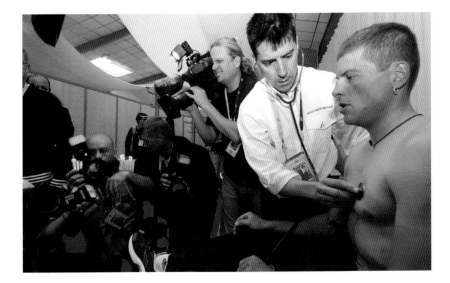

Cycling and the culture of doping

Doping—the use of illegal performance-enhancing drugs—has dogged
professional cycling from its earliest years. Pharmacological knowledge has
moved on somewhat since the beginning of the twentieth century, when
riders sometimes resorted to alcohol, cocaine and even strychnine—all
toxic and of dubious performance-enhancing properties—perhaps mainly
to anaesthetise themselves from the rigours of the road with a temporary
hit of euphoria. Amphetamines, which had been made widely available
to troops during the second world war, became the drugs of choice in the
pro peloton from the 1950s onwards. There was no anti-doping agency
or testing regime, and the governing bodies chose to turn a blind eye—in
an attitude that can be summed up as "this sport is too hard on the riders,
so whatever it takes...". The great French cyclist of the 1960s, five-time
Tour winner Jacques Anquetil, once asked sardonically if people seriously
expected riders to race in the Tour de France 'on mineral water alone'. It took
the death of British cyclist Tommy Simpson, who collapsed on the slopes of
Mont Ventoux in 1967 of heart failure brought on by heat exhaustion and
dehydration exacerbated by alcohol and amphetamine use, before the issue
of doping and dope testing was taken seriously. Urine tests were introduced,
although it was not long before riders found ingenious ways of cheating—
smuggling clean urine samples in to the controls. There is an apocryphal tale
of the cyclist who was called back after a test, after he'd submitted a vial of
his wife's urine as it it were his, to be told that his sample was certainly clear
of illegal substances—but that he did appear to be pregnant.

   In the 1970s, a new class of drugs began to appear: anabolic steroids.
Amphetamines were useful for cycling only in limited ways. They did not
provide an instrinsic performance benefit, but they did suppress a cyclist's
subjective feelings of fatigue—they enabled a rider to push himself beyond
his usual limits. This could be very effective in one-day races, of course, but

there was always a payback—the rider would be wiped out with exhaustion and need several days to recover. Thus, their utility for stage races was very limited, in effect an act of ultimately counter-productive desperation. But steroids—a class of drugs originally developed at the end of the war to help concentration camp victims recover from the effects of starvation—had been pioneered behind the Iron Curtain by Eastern European athletes in strength-based sports such as weight-lifting because drugs such as testosterone helped build lean body mass (i.e. muscle). For an endurance athlete, the benefit is less clear—riders do not want big muscles: strength is useful, but bulk is not in a sport where weight is a crucial issue. However, if correctly administered, steroids can help a cyclist increase the ratio of lean muscle mass to fat, and more importantly, can aid recovery by boosting the body's ability to repair itself after heavy training.

How widespread steroid abuse became in cycling is not clear, but by the mid 1980s the testing regime had to a large extent caught up with the cheats and a urine test was available. In the 1988 Tour de France, the top Dutch rider, Gert-Jan Theunisse, was penalised for testing positive for an anabolic steroid. This was a significant scalp for the testers, but the big one got away: the overall crown was won that year by the Spanish rider Pedro Delgado amid highly controversial circumstances in which he tested positive not for a banned substance but for a masking agent. While this substance was not yet illegal, and Delgado vigorously denied doping, it is hard to imagine why a rider would be taking a masking agent if not to conceal the use of an illegal performance-enhancing drug. The masking agent was added to the banned list shortly afterwards.

But by then steroids were about to become irrelevant: within a couple of years, rumours were sweeping the pro peloton of an amazing new drug that could boost a rider's performance by ten to 15 per cent—an incredible margin of effect, and far more than a rider could hope to achieve by even the most rigorous training programme. That drug was erythropoietin, commonly known as EPO. EPO was developed, as most drugs banned for athletes are, for a legitimate medical use—in this case, for kidney dialysis patients. The process of dialysis damaged the patients' red blood cells, causing severe anaemia; EPO was administered because it mimics the body's own hormone that instructs the bone marrow to produce more red blood cells. Give the same drug to a healthy athlete, and his body will develop an unusual amount of red blood cells, boosting the oxygen-carrying capacity of his blood. A similar effect can be gained legally by training at altitude—the thinner air stimulates the body to up its red blood cell count—but only to a limited degree. EPO was so effective it could turn second-rate riders into world-beaters.

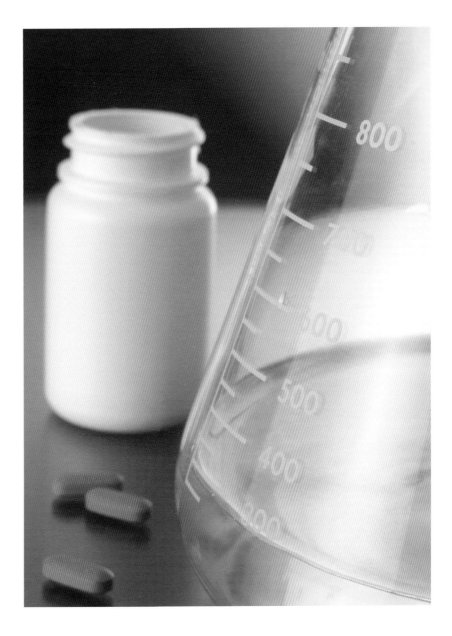

The early 1990s were a period of apparent crisis in French cycling—no squad based in France seemed to be able to win a race. They were scarcely picking up minor places even. With hindsight, the French teams were underperforming not because France no longer produced any talented cyclists, but because they were either too ethical or too slow in the uptake to medicate their riders with EPO as many of the Italian, Spanish and Dutch teams, we now know, were. Some finally succumbed—and it was an entire French team, Festina, that was finally caught in 1998 when, on the eve of the Tour de France, a team soigneur was stopped on the French-Dutch border by customs officials who discovered a huge cache of illegal performance-enhancing drugs, including EPO, in the boot of his car.

The EPO explosion took its toll in other ways. In the early 1990s in Holland, where cycle racing is so popular that there is a thriving domestic professional and semi-pro scene, there were a string of unexplained deaths of Dutch riders who seemed to have suffered mysterious heart failure in their sleep. The generally accepted hypothesis now is that these racers had discovered EPO and were self-medicating without realising the risks of excessive dosages. The immediate danger with EPO (and there are other longer-term health concerns) is that the increased red blood cell count makes the blood thicker, leading to a risk of clotting or of the heart failing because it can no longer pump the artificially haemaglobin-rich sludge the blood has become.

The problem for cycling was that it took the anti-doping regime a decade to come up with a straightforward and reliable test for EPO: not until 2000 was this measure brought in. Until then, an absurd situation obtained where the sport's governing body, the Union Cycliste International (UCI), merely established a limit for the percentage composition of blood that is red blood cells (the rest being plasma) of 50 per cent—known as the haematocrit level. A level of 50 per cent is very high—but could just conceivably be achieved by an elite athlete who had trained at altitude, without dope-cheating. In practice what this meant was that riders were carefully medicated by a team doctor to achieve a 49 per cent haematocrit level—and why bother to go to the trouble and expense of altitude training when there's a convenient pill. In the absence of an EPO test, it was, in effect, officially licensed doping.

Since 2000, several high-profile cyclists have fallen foul either of the anti-doping agencies or of magistrates investigating large scale, organised cheating among coaches and cyclists. The testing regime seems tighter, and so the sport cleaner. But there is no cause for complacency: the lesson of the recent past is that the dope-cheats and their crooked pharmacists are constantly on the search for some new substance, as yet undetectable, that will give an athlete the edge in what is a big money sport.

Cycle sport: the best of the rest

Track racing

The velodrome has been a feature of cycle sport for over a century. From the 1890s, a time when many roads were unmade and most others cobbled, a track provided the best surface, smooth and fast, for racing. While cycling was still a novelty and people were fascinated by the speed of these human-powered vehicles, the velodrome was a source of popular entertainment. Steeply banked wooden tracks could be disassembled, hauled around and reassembled in the next big city all over Europe, North America, and further afield. The track athletes were itinerant performers, much like a circus troupe. People came in droves to watch extraordinary events such as 24 hour races–and bet on the outcome.

The closest we have today to this form of the sport are the winter 'sixes' that take place in Germany, Switzerland, France, Holland and Belgium: a series of six-day events, combining all sorts of races, watched by a convivial crowd enjoying action-packed racing at close quarters–and, in Ghent for instance, plenty of Belgian beer as well.

The velodrome has also long figured as the venue for one of the key Olympic cycling disciplines. The events themselves have varied over time, but the main elements today are: the pursuit, the sprints, and the points race and Madison. In a pursuit, two riders (or two teams of riders, in the case of the team pursuit) set off from opposite sides of the track, each ostensibly pursuing the other in an effort to catch him over a distance of four kilometres (three kilometres for women). In fact, at the elite level where races are often decided by tenths if not hundredths of seconds, it is relatively unusual for one to overhaul the other, and the race is, in effect, each against the clock. But there is an added tactical interest: often, for example, one rider will make a fast start, but then struggle to hold the pace, while his rival relentlessly claws back the advantage.

Sprints also come in various formats, but for the spectators it is a chance to see a completely different type of athlete. While the pursuiters are lean time triallists, tuned to execute a maximal aerobic effort for rather less than four-and-a-half minutes, sprinters are bulky, massively muscled types, more like body-builders or weight-lifters than cyclists, who are trained to concentrate their explosive power in a burst lasting only a few seconds, a couple of laps at most. They are sheer strength and pure speed, but their game is also one of guile and wiles, courage and nerve. Sprints can be some of the most exciting viewing in the velodrome.

The Madison and points races are for cyclists who look physically more like road racers, and some 'roadies' turn their hand very effectively to the track; but they need to be the sort of rider who has a real turn of speed. The Madison is one of the most spectacular events to watch, because riders work in pairs. Only one of each team of two is racing at any one time, while the other rests, slowly circling the track above the red line; they swap roles by playing tag—but with a special technique known as a handsling where the faster one imparts his momentum to the slower one, and flings him back in to the action. With riders all over the track, moving at different speeds, and swapping in and out, it is deeply confusing to score, but also rather beautiful to watch. The points race is a more conventional event in which riders can gain points in sprints every set number of laps; it is a trial of tactical sense, but also of supreme speed and fitness.

Track racing has made something of a comeback in the UK after many decades of slow decline and the closure of several older venues. A new velodrome in Manchester has provided an Olympic standard facility suitable for world class competition; another has since been built in Newport, South Wales, while the 2012 Olympics will bequeath yet another to central London. British riders have excelled on the track, beginning with Chris Boardman's gold in the individual pursuit at Barcelona in 1992 and culminating with an impressive haul of medals at Athens in 2004, with Bradley Wiggins winning a hat-trick of gold, silver and bronze medals. These achievements have led to several years of consistent investment in British cyclists, creating a virtuous circle of sporting success. With road-racing and time-trialling ever more difficult to organise on Britain's congested roads, it is hard not to be persuaded by the logic that the future for British cycle sport is based primarily on the track.

Mountain biking and cyclo-cross

Since the 1980s, mountain biking has become an extremely popular version of recreational cycling, and a vibrant field of competition also. The technology of mountain bikes is constantly improving—features such as hydraulic disc brakes and 'intelligent' suspension are top of the range one year and then on budget bikes the next. The performance of modern bikes is staggering compared to even a decade ago. It is a market driven by innovation, and that is because people continue to spend lots of money on mountain biking.

There is lots of off-road racing available for amateurs. As a scene, it has quite a different style and tone from the older, more traditional forms of road-racing. It feels younger and hipper, its subculture more akin to the skateboarding or surfing fraternity. In many ways, it is more accessible and less exclusive as a world—and that openness has attracted plenty of talent. Britain has its share of world-class riders, although we haven't yet landed the world or Olympic titles that the 'trackies' have.

Above: photograph by Dean Taylor.

There are several types of mountain bike racing. The classic form of the sport is 'cross-country' (XC for short): a race run over laps of an off-road circuit, which will include some tough climbs, some fast descents, and lots of technical tests. The object is to cover a given distance (a certain number of laps) in the shortest possible time. Top mountain bikers are extremely fit athletes, and in the recent past some have made successful transitions to the highest levels of road cycling, but a great deal of their speed off-road comes from their supreme handling skills. Choosing the right line down a precipitous descent or weaving the most rapid route through a gnarly piece of singletrack, littered with rocks and tree roots, leaves no room for error or fear. Another form of cross-country competition involves 'enduro' events—over long distances point-to-point, and even over several stages. There is even a thriving scene of night racing, where mountain bikers race around a circuit using powerful lights to see their way. In general, where road racing can be seen as tradition-bound and conservative, the mountain biking scene is less hide-bound, more gung-ho. To many, this 'just do it' ethic is a breath of fresh air; there's more an attitude of 'if you want to race, just bring your bike and ride'.

Cross-country mountain biking is also a hugely popular leisure activity. Wherever there are trails and bridlepaths, they'll see considerable traffic of weekend mountain bikers, out to enjoy the countryside and a fun, healthy outdoor activity with plenty of thrills and kicks on offer. It has become so widespread that, in certain national parks for example, mountain biking has had to be restricted because the knobbly tyres can cause erosion in environmentally sensitive areas.

Downhill

Cross-country titles have the most prestige at the Olympics and World Championships but there is growing participation and interest in 'downhill' racing. Downhill bikes have evolved away from the conventional cross-country mountain bike. Since there is no premium in weight-saving, because the only object is to cover a long technical descent as fast as possible, downhill bikes are very heavy but extremely strong pieces of kit. Their suspension forks also have much more 'travel' (that is, they can compress further, taking bigger hits), and are raked at a shallower angle—closer in design to moto-cross bikes. The disc brakes need to be very powerful and the suspension extremely resilient. The speeds top racers reach on these machines over viciously rough terrain is terrifying—up to 70-80 kilometres per hour. As with moto-cross riders, substantial body armour, including a full-face helmet, is de rigeuer. Again, whereas in so many cycling disciplines weight-saving is an obsession, in downhilling carrying extra weight is actually an advantage—because gravity equals speed. Not for the faint-hearted, downhill definitely justifies its tag as an extreme sport. You might see it as somewhere between surfing and skiing—only it probably hurts more if you fall off. It definitely has the adrenaline factor.

Freeriding

A related mountain biking discipline, which is nurtured by a growing scene, is 'freeriding': it is very similar to downhill, involving a rapid descent down a hair-raisingly mountainous course. The difference is that points are awarded by judges for style and 'artistic merit', rather than just for speed against the clock. Whereas XC and downhill racers tend to keep at least one wheel on the ground most of the time, because they need the traction and control, in freeriding 'getting air' is definitely a good thing. In that and other respects, it shares some cross-over elements with stunt-riding bike sports such as BMX, dirt-jumping, street/urban, and trials.

Trials

Trialling is another bike sport modelled on a similar motorbike discipline. Bikes with either 20 inch (BMX) or 26 inch (mountain bike) wheels can be used. Riders have to perform complex manoeuvres involving hops, jumps and balances, over a series of vertiginous obstacles—anything from planks and oil drums to concrete blocks. Street/urban tends to occupy a 'found environment' closer to what skateboarders would use:

ramps, half-pipes and railings where a dizzying array of tricks can be displayed—complex sequences of acrobatic jumps and grinds. Bikes with 20 inch wheels and very small, low frames are used for this kind of stunt riding. In all these spin-offs from BMX and mountain biking, the 'look' is very important: these are youth cultures as much as sporting disciplines. Ultra-baggy trousers worn low, baggy T-shirts, hoodies, beanies or baseball caps... this is biking as a statement in urban cool.

Cyclo-cross

Cyclo-cross is pretty traditional by comparison. It has a much longer pedigree than mountain biking, being a longstanding form of off-road winter racing chiefly for road cyclists. The cyclo-cross bike resembles a racing bike, but with cantilever brakes and more clearance around the wheels to allow for the accumulation of mud and with knobbly tyres for off-road grip. Although a 'niche' form of cycle sport, it is popular in northern Europe and north America (Lance Armstrong has been known to turn out for cyclo-cross races in the off-season). Above all, it has a huge following in Belgium, where crowds of tens of thousands turn out to watch their local heroes blast round tough, technical circuits of mixed tarmac, dirt trail, muddy fields and sand dunes. Britain has produced some notable 'crossers' (the Discovery Channel professional Roger Hammond was a junior world champion), but the international top level is dominated by the Belgians.

The racing usually lasts only an hour or so, but the tricky conditions make for plenty of thrills and spills and good spectating. The riders have not only their fitness, speed and strength tested, but also their handling skills and their ability to negotiate technical challenges such as steps and hurdles. Sometimes riders have to dismount and shoulder their bikes, or they will try to 'bunny-hop' obstacles such as felled tree trunks. Not surprisingly, many mountain bikers transfer to cyclo-cross in the winter and compete very successfully.

Because most cyclo-cross and mountain biking races are relatively short, many can be put on at the same venue in the course of a day, banded by age, sex and experience. It is fine to turn up and give it a go, and no one cares if you don't have the latest gear, a team jersey, or even the right shoes. If you have a bike and you want to try it out, you can enter and just do your best. It's a friendly, informal scene—and a good way into cycle sport.

Cyclosportives

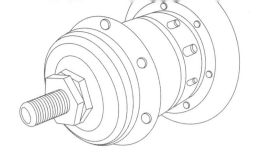

If the story of the 1980s and 90s was the mountain bike boom, then the twenty-first century has seen something of a comeback for the racing bike. There is so much choice and the quality is now so good. One of the reasons for this resurgence is the growing popularity of cyclosportives. These are rides that are not races, but riders do 'compete' in time trials. There is no set time, but sometimes there is a graded standard (a gold medal time, silver and so on). They are often quite long, from 100-200 kilometres typically, and over challenging terrain. For many who take part, the satisfaction comes from merely finishing the course.

The 'Grande Trophée' series in France consists of an entire season of events, and some take in the monumental landmarks that regularly feature in the Tour de France—mountains such as Mont Ventoux and epic climbs such as Alpe d'Huez. Some people aim to complete the whole series—and will compete for an overall result—but many pick and choose the events they fancy. Italy has a parallel series of Gran Fondo events. The greatest cyclosportive of them all is l'Etape du Tour—essentially, an amateur stage of the Tour de France, run over the same closed roads enjoyed by the professionals and up the same Alpine or Pyrenean climbs, but a few days before the Tour proper arrives. The thrill is that you too can suffer on the same road to Calvary—and then see that the pros will ride the 200 kilometres it took you virtually all day to cover in about five hours. The Etape has become so popular that more people enter than can be accommodated; but it is a wonderful experience and worth trying at least once.

You do not need to travel abroad to take part in cyclosportives. They are increasingly becoming a feature of the domestic cycling scene, and they are justly becoming ever more popular as a perfect alternative for people who love cycling for fitness but who do not want to race. The attraction of these events is that there is always help at hand, if you need food, water or mechanical assistance; there is a start and a finish and appropriate ceremony attached; and, above all, the company of lots of other cyclists, which also makes the roads feel safer. For those who wish to treat these rides as quasi-races, they are plenty challenging enough; but they are not so daunting as to exclude a much larger intermediate class of rider. And there is the strong social theme—for cyclists enjoy nothing so much as a good chat after a ride to talk about just how hard it was!

ME AND MY BIKE

I only tell my close friends,
and they think it's really good.

Lucy Garner / UK

Lucy Garner is a normal, ten year old primary school student in Leicester. A few years ago, her dad entered her into a cyclo-cross race and she discovered she had something of a knack for cycling. In fact she has since won the title of British Shcools National Champion in no less than six different types of cycling; cyclo-cross, hard track, grass track, roller racing, circuit racing and time trials, and is currently the National Under-10s Cycling Champion.

It's not easy maintaining that level of expertise. She trains two days a week on Tuesdays and Fridays and races on both Saturday and Sunday. Luckily primary school is not terribly demanding in terms of homework.

Although cyclo-cross is probably Lucy's favourite type of cycling, she also enjoys riding her penny farthing and is a member of the Desford Lane Pedallers Veteran Cycle Club (as well as the Leicester off-road club).

Since her success in the National Championships, Lucy has become the poster-girl for Leicester City Council in their Be Seen on A Bike Campaign. Despite this publicity and her success in her field, Lucy keeps her achievements quiet: "I only tell my close friends and they think it is really good."

The number of kilometres we cover depends on how many pubs we stop at on the way...

Raoul Morley / UK

Opposite: Photograph by Dean Taylor.

There are lots of things Raoul likes about mountain biking. He likes being outside, he likes the adrenaline, he enjoys the exercise, and not least, he likes the social aspect of it. Unlike the regimented discipline of road riding, mountain biking can be a very laid back, friendly sport. Every week, Raoul will meet up with a group of cyclists from all over the country at Waterloo Station, get on the train to a pre-arranged destination and will cycle all day, sometimes covering in excess of 50 kilometres (although frequent pub stops mean that this is open to variation).

Raoul has been into mountain biking since he was fourteen. He remembers picking up a copy of MBUK and immediately keying into the look and feel of the sport. He started racing when he was 18, and dropped out because he didn't relate to the competitive aspect of it. He picked it up again when he lived in a town just outside Durham, in the north of the country, commuting 20 miles off road to and from work each day. When he moved down to London, he got in touch with an online community of mountain bikers, joined a ride, and has been cycling with them ever since. It's a friendly bunch of people and they meet regularly in a social as well as a sporting capacity. Raoul confesses that there is a high quotient of geekiness amongst mountain bikers, and in fact 70 per cent of the people he rides with work in IT. This means that if you are looking for a mountain biking group to join, online forums are the best way to get in touch with people.

Raoul rides a custom built, single speed mountain bike with no suspension. This is a fairly unusual choice, and causes some serious muscle ache—but he likes the challenge. There are those who will even ride fixed gear mountain bikes, but he says this is one step too far. However, in the city, commuting to work, he will ride one of two fixed geared bikes, his custom built pride and joy (which he calls 'bling fixie') or the rather more basic track bike that he bought off a friend for £50 (the 'beast'). He is happy to commute around London on them during the week, but he freely admits that if he doesn't go for at least one major ride out in the country at the weekend, he gets seriously bad-tempered.

Moving forward

So the bicycle is back. The wheel has turned and, once more, its time has come again. But the modern world is a very different place to the way it was in Victorian glory days, and governments, manufacturers and individuals need to acknowledge the realities of today's climate. Policies, equipment and attitudes have to accommodate the changing requirements of a world in which the car reigns supreme.

Because the bicycle is clean and green, compared with other modes of transport, it matches the new environmental criteria that transport professionals, traffic engineers and town planners have to work with. Whilst motor vehicles have increasingly come to be regarded as a problem—the cause of casualties, congestion and carbon dioxide emissions—which has to be tackled with a growing raft of measures like traffic calming, speed cameras, road-pricing and so on, cycling is seen by policy-makers as part of the solution.

This is no surprise to the campaigners and the people who have been using their bikes as their main form of transport for years. Cyclists tend, as a rule, to be rationalists. Which is not to say that they are better than other people (apart from anything, that would be manifestly untrue); nor are they necessarily more reasonable than others (just look at the quite vicious internal controversies that go on, for instance, over such subjects as bike helmets). But once someone is converted to regular cycle use, its logic becomes so clear and compelling that it does in some way make rationalists of us all. The bicycle is so obviously the answer to some of our most pressing social problems. Worried about greenhouse gases and want to save the planet? Ride a bike instead of using your car. Worried about your lack of fitness and inability to keep up the gym habit? Cancel the astronomical membership fee and just ride a bike to work. Worried about your children's lack of activity and that they might soon be joining the grim statistics about juvenile obesity? Get them into going to school by bike.

The social logic of cycle use is best demonstrated in the figures for cycle use in Europe—especially the countries with a strong tradition of social democracy: Germany, Holland, Denmark and Scandinavia. So are we seeing the United Kingdom and the United States getting on their bikes to join them?

Yes and no. It is very hard to imagine that cycling in the US and the UK will ever reach the same levels of prestige that it enjoys in some parts of northern Europe. And although governments often talk a good game about road safety, traffic restraint and encouraging people to think about he alternatives to private car use, they often lack the political will to challenge the oil industry and the motoring lobby. Neither countries appear to be doing anything to disincentivise the galloping sales of vastly inefficient 4x4 vehicles, and both seem to be investing heavily in the construction of new roads (a vast hidden subsidy for motorists).

On the up side, local governments in specific counties and states in Britain and America have taken matters into their own hands. In London, for example, careful investment by the mayor into cycling has resulted in an extraordinary increase in cycle use—up 100 per cent from 2000 to 2005—making it a flagship for what can be achieved. Even in an unpromising environment, where there is huge competition for road-space, serious investment combined with political will delivers results. Spending on cycling has now reached £24 million ($42 million) a year in Greater London, which begins to place it on a par for per capita expenditure with many of the European cities which have achieved high rates of cycle use.

It is impossible to overstate what a significant development this is for cycling campaigners. Many of them spent long years in the wilderness struggling to get the smallest concessions and the most minimal provision through the bureaucracy of local government. Then they faced the paradox of bad infrastructure: they had to go on making the argument for more cycle lanes and cycle routes when council officers pointed out that people weren't using the ones they'd already paid for (because they were badly designed and didn't link up, of course). The implications of seeing the tide finally turning decisively in its favour is something that, perhaps, the cycling lobby has not yet fully got its head around, so ingrained are the mental habits of being embattled outsiders.

London may be the flagship of Britain's bike-friendly future, but some lesser known centres of bicycle culture look set to join it. Darlington in the northeast, for instance, recently became one of six towns in Britain to be selected as a "cycling demonstration town", designed to set an example of how to transform urban sprawls into two-wheeled havens (the others are Aylesbury, Brighton, Derby, Exeter and Lancaster). Under this scheme, run by Cycling England and part-funded by the Department for Transport (DfT) with matching cash from each local authority, the six towns will get one million pounds ($1.7 million) a year for three years, all to be spent on promoting cycle use. In Darlington, cycling's share of the annual transport budget would normally be £150,000 ($260,000). Suddenly, these towns will be getting investment on a par with the best in mainland Europe. The bulk of the money will go on putting in new infrastructure, but the funding will also e put towards paying for teams of consultants to make door-to-door calls on every household in the town (of 100,000 inhabitants) to offer personal travel plans. These won't necessarily involve cycling; they might provide information about bus routes and timetables, for example. But the marketing effort will strongly encourage people to try cycling—pointing out the new, safer routes being installed, providing handy cycle maps, even offering discounts on bikes and cycling gear at local shops.

Darlington's level of cycle use is right on the national average, with about two per cent of all journeys being done by bike. The target is to raise this to at least five to six per cent in the three years. That might not sound a dramatic shift, but it would make Darlington a visibly different place—its centre more appealing to pedestrians as well as cyclists, the immediate periphery much less dominated by private car traffic. The larger, longer-term vision would be to demonstrate that European levels of funding of pro-cycling measures will reliably bring European levels of cycle use. It's not as if the British are in some way genetically indisposed to riding bikes; just fifty years ago, after all, 12 million people in the UK were regular cyclists. The premise is that, with a decent budget, a situation in which the urban environment has been planned and built in such a way as positively to discourage cycling and promote private car use can be reversed.

CYCLING IN EUROPE
Km/yr/head of population

Integration initiatives

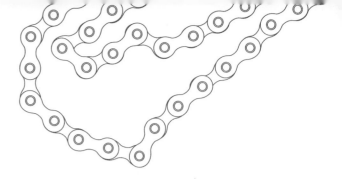

Below: a bicycle carriage on a California train.

Britain is still a long way behind other countries in terms of transport integration. In many US cities, for example, modern buses are designed either to carry bicycles on external racks or to allow passengers to mount the bus with a bike. In the UK, rail transport is a very significant segment of commuting travel, and one where the opportunities to develop synergies between bike and train are obvious. Yet the commercial pressures on rail operators to fill carriages with as many passengers as possible, while cutting the number of staff required on trains and platforms, has led to cyclists being designed out of the equation in the new rolling stock: the old guard vans that could easily hold half a dozen bikes have gone. Anything but folding bikes have been banned by many operators at peak times on rush-hour routes. And even on scheduled inter-city services, cyclists are obliged to make a reservation prior to travel in order to be permitted to bring a bike on board. Needless to say, these things are somewhat run differently in many of European countries. In Germany, for instance, it may be necessary to book your bike onto a train, but on local services it is common to find entire cars devoted to bicycle carriage. Bikes can also be taken on to buses and trams except at peak commuting hours.

Above: the Bycyklen public bike scheme in Århus, Denmark.

One future measure that is creating a great deal of interest in Europe is the new bike pool schemes. The idea in itself is not new. Amsterdam, with some claim to be the world capital of cycling, pioneered such a scheme in the 1960s with its 'white bikes'. The scheme—bikes that anyone could just pick up, hop on, ride across town, hop off and park, at virtually no cost—sounded almost too utopian to work. And that partly proved the case: these early bike pools were badly hit by theft and vandalism. But the basic idea was too good ever to have gone away completely. Copenhagen runs a very successful city bike operation, now in its 11th year. Because it runs from April to December, but not in the harshest winter months, the 'Bycyklen' scheme is particularly a boon for tourists, who simply pay a refundable £2 ($3.50) coin deposit to release one of the 2,000 bikes from the 100 plus bike parks distributed around the inner urban area. The bikes are well maintained by a team of mobile repair shops.

More exciting still as a model for how such schemes could work elsewhere (perhaps in less prosperous and bike-friendly places than Copenhagen) is the French city of Lyons' Vélo'V initiative. Originally explored on a smaller scale in Vienna, the beauty of this new type of bike pooling arrangement is that it is subscription-based: people have to sign up by registering their credit card details and paying a 150 Euro deposit, which is claimed if the bike is not returned within 24 hours; in return, they get a swipe card and PIN number to access the bikes. In other words, people have an incentive in using the bike responsibly; and there is a penalty for abusing the system.

Vélo'V subscribers pay a modest hourly rental charge, but the first half-hour is free—and most people's journeys fall inside that time. The scheme makes brilliant use of new technology in other ways: any attempt to steal bikes from the purpose-built racks sets off an alarm, while electronic sensors check the roadworthiness of the bike (that the lights are working, the tyres have enough pressure, etc) and communicate its condition to a central bureau. The Vélo'V scheme was such an instant hit that the computer system had to be upgraded to deal with demand within hours of its launch. And now, less than a year after it started, Vélo'V has 20,000 subscribers (in a city of about 1 million), and 2,000 bikes rented from nearly 200 stations around Lyons. The plan is to expand the scale to 4,000 bikes in 2007. The only significant teething problem encountered is that people tend to ride the bikes downhill more, leaving the stations in higher parts of the city depleted, so that JC Decaux, the company running the scheme on behalf of the city authority, has to take measures to redistribute the distinctive red and silver bicycles.

If it can work so successfully in Lyons, there is no reason why the Vélo'V model could not function equally well in almost any town or city in Europe. Even, perhaps, in Britain—although it remains to be seen whether the security measures of the Vélo'V scheme would be sufficient to deter our incredibly industrious bike thieves, responsible for well over 100,000 thefts per year.

Secure futures

Theft is a huge problem. Police estimate that perhaps only a quarter of bike thefts are reported, making the true figure as high as half a million a year. One estimate says that 17 per cent of cyclists experience theft every year. With losses running so high, insurance premiums are correspondingly exorbitant—varying from ten per cent to 20 per cent of the replacement value of the bike per year. Yet the greatest cost of bike theft is a social, rather than a financial, one: one study has found that nearly a quarter of those who have a bike stolen stop cycling altogether, while for a massive two-thirds the experience is so dispiriting (and inconvenient) that they report cycling less as a result.

There are few locks that can resist the well-equipped and determined thief for more than a few minutes. No one has yet come up with an electronic tracking device for the bike, although an online registration scheme, which has helped to cut mobile phone theft, has now been established for bikes in the UK. Whether this proves successful in restoring stolen bikes to their owners is another matter; there is plenty of anecdotal evidence from aggrieved cyclists who have found their stolen bicycle on sale at a dodgy street market stall that it is remarkably difficult to get police officers interested in this particular form of stolen goods. A more promising development is the innovative approach of the Design Against Crime research centre at Central St Martin's College, where a designer has come up with a prototype bicycle that can be locked by releasing and refastening a metal rod which also operates as the down tube. The only way to steal the bike is to cut this rod, but if that is done the bike loses the bracing of the rod/down tube and becomes structurally unstable, thus effectively worthless. This clever piece of design has yet to be developed as a commercial product, but the idea would dovetail perfectly with a bike pool scheme.

New technologies

Other innovations in the pipeline could include bar-mounted GPS satellite navigation systems. Handheld devices for walkers and cyclists are already on the market, although they remain pricey at present. Although the streetmaps may be handy for urban cyclists, these mini satellite navigation systems may prove more popular with mountain bikers making use of the growing number of trails and tracks being developed in UK forestry areas to attract recreational cyclists.

Other gadgetry on its way is more predictable. Hydraulic operation of brakes is already replacing wire cables in mountain bikes and hybrids. How far this goes depends on the cost and reliability. Wires are extremely light and dependable, even if the technology is a century old. They also have the advantage of being relatively simple to maintain at home by the DIY mechanic, who is likely to be stumped, on the other hand, by a hydraulic system. The one main drawback of the old-fashioned steel wire is a susceptibility to rust and stick inside their cable sleeves, which is what has made the hydraulic option for bikes that often get muddy or wet particularly appealing.

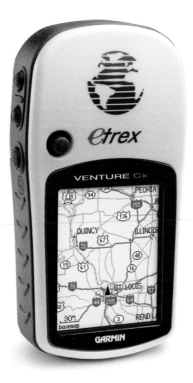

Electronic control of gear shifting is also being piloted on professional road bikes. So far, the signs are very positive: shifts are said to be far faster than with the conventional cable-operated system. But power, reliability and weight will be issues to be resolved, since each derailleur on the bike will require small electric servo motors to push the mechanical element of the derailleur. And anything electrical and electronic on a bike will have to prove itself capable of resisting all weathers. As any racing cyclist or mountain biker will know, there is virtually nowhere that sand, grit and water will not get after several hours on the road on a really wet day. If damp grit can get in your ears and up your nose (literally), then it's a safe bet that it will also find itself way inside the gear-shift mechanism. With such technical challenges involved, it may take several years before the component manufacturers can roll out a budget-priced 'diffusion range' of electronic shifting systems for the sort of bikes people buy in the high street.

Carbon-fibre composites look set to be the material of the future. The way the fibres are set in resinous compounds mean that extremely efficient and aerodynamic shapes can be moulded; the result is a frame that is light, stiff, very strong yet shock-absorbent—as close to an ideal range of properties for a bike frame as can presently be imagined. And not just the frame: there is scarcely anything on a top-end road or mountain bike that cannot be found in carbon-fibre: cranks, handlebars, chainrings, seatposts, derailleurs, even saddles. A lot of this trend is down to fashion: put simply, carbon is sexy. The distinctive look of the carbon-fibre weave has already become such a powerful signifier of high

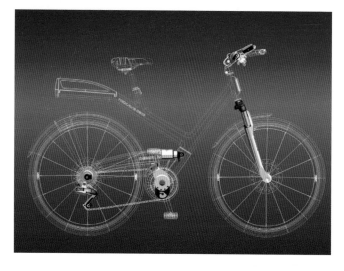

Above: the Shimano Smoover electronic
gear shift system, also known as DI2.

performance that it has been mimicked by everything from non-carbon (carbon 'wannabe') bike parts to cycling websites. Prices have been coming down as the bike trade gears up to the growing demand: it is now possible to buy a well-specced bike with full carbon frame and forks for under £1,000 ($1,700). The mass market is still supplied by aluminium frames, and that is such a huge production system that it will be some time before carbon replaces aluminium in the millions of budget bikes made every year. But as the popular brands try to meet consumers' aspirations to have a carbon bike at ever more competitive prices, production is bound to shift. The use of desirable, cutting edge materials also has an important symbolic dimension: it means that people think of the bike as part of our collective future, rather than something quaint and antique belonging to the past.

Bicycle culture has received a boost, too. As with so many special interest groups, the internet has proved a hugely powerful tool for putting people with a common enthusiasm in touch with one another, and for providing and disseminating information—for all kinds of cyclists, from sports and recreational riders, to commuters and campaigners. Threads in cycling chatrooms positively hum with electronic dialogue, while the business of finding obscure bike bits and buying and selling stuff has been revolutionised by online retailing and auction sites like eBay. The resurgence of interest in cycling has spawned creative offshoots such as a bicycle film festival, which has now become an international annual event touring cities in the US, Australia and Europe.

Where do we go from here?

The bike may be back, and in some areas, at least, more people are cycling, but it is much too soon for any triumphalism. A wider variety of people—more women, certainly; in some areas, more members of ethnic minorities; and, thanks to the growth in cycle training in schools, more children. But there is little to be complacent about. The greatest growth in transport is still in motor traffic. The curve runs inexorably upwards: traffic has nearly doubled since 1980 (while the number of private cars on the road has gone up by 75 per cent); the rate of growth has slowed, but has nonetheless risen by 21 per cent since 1990. The only silver lining is that congestion in Greater London, for instance, has seen average traffic speeds drop below 25 kilometres per hour. But it's a pretty dark cloud when you stop to consider that the concept of average speed conceals the fact that many drivers, frustrated by having to wait in long queues, accelerate well past the statutory speed limit in order to reach the next bottleneck quicker. A reduced average speed does not necessarily make the roads safer for cyclists; and congestion doesn't really help anybody.

Meanwhile, the long-term trend for cycling is still running in the other direction. According to the latest figures from the Department for Transport, the average distance cycled every year per capita has risen very slightly since 2002 (to a mere 57 kilometres), but is still less than it was a decade ago. The aggregate number of 'passenger kilometres' travelled in Britain per year by bike is stuck obstinately where it has been since the early 1990s, at four billion, which means that cycling's 'modal share' remains at one per cent of all journeys (if air travel is factored in; two per cent if not). Any growth in cycling seems, as yet, too local and small in scale to show up in the big picture.

The single most often cited reason for not cycling is a perception that cycling is unsafe. Yet the actual risk of serious harm is incredibly low. In 2004 (the last year for which figures are available), 134 cyclists were killed on British roads. This is 134 too many fatalities, of course, but what does that number mean in relative terms? Well, the unpleasant truth is that a transport casualties statistician might call 134 deaths an average month for motorists—a total of 1,671 car users were killed in 2004.

Absolute numbers, though, can be misleading: a better measure is the frequency of casualties occurring. By distance travelled, cars look safer, with 2.7 deaths per billion passenger kilometre (public transport is better still: 0.2 for buses; 0.1 for trains). Cyclists are killed at a rate of 25 per billion kilometres but then most cyclists do far less mileage

Below: in Jaipur, India, cycling remains the primary form of transport. Photograph by Paul van Roekel and Anja de Graaf.

than motorists. So, although I clock up 8,000 kilometres a year by bike, which is much more than average, I'd need to live 5,000 years to stand an odds-on chance of dying on my bike. And I am extremely untypical, when you consider the average distance travelled per person by bicycle per year (as above, 57 kilometres). One actuarial estimate reckons that the average cyclist could ride for 20,000 years before coming a cropper. What is certain is that the minuscule risk of serious injury is far outweighed by the health benefits of cycling—the cardiovascular fitness that boosts your immune system, wards off disease and illness, and even postpones the effects of ageing. According to one study, the value of just 30 minutes a day of moderate exercise on a bike means that the gains in increased life span outstrip years lost through accident fatalities by a ratio of 20 to one.

What is also certain is that the more people cycle, the better other road users adjust, and so the safer it is. The statistics illustrate this clearly: in the UK just 2.3 per cent of journeys are done by bike; in Denmark, 18 per cent; and in Holland a remarkable 25 per cent. And respectively, while British cyclists risk becoming a casualty at the rate of eight per 100 million kilometres, the figure in Denmark is just one per 100 million kilometres, and in The Netherlands it's 0.8. The Dutch cycle on average about 850 kilometres per person per year (fifteen-fold more than we do), yet Holland records only twice as many cycling fatalities for all those billions of extra kilometres.

According to transport policy research, there is a tipping point at about four per cent of modal share where the sheer volume of cyclists on the road becomes inescapably noticeable and begins to alter the environment. A critical mass, you might say, is then reached, where cycling becomes a central rather than a marginal mode of transport, shifting the traffic priorities irreversibly. Getting to a mere four per cent may not sound like a huge challenge, but it means doubling the number of people cycling every day. Infrastructure can help achieve that transformation, indeed it cannot happen without it, but this also means a cultural revolution where the bike becomes a natural part of ordinary people's daily lives.

Once it has become part of your way of life, it becomes almost unthinkable not to ride a bike. The bicycle becomes almost a physical part of you—as if, as the surrealist Irish writer Flann O'Brien imagined in The Third Policeman, you exchanged atoms and became half-bike, half-person. It's that modern unity of man and machine that so excited the first generation of Victorian cyclists about the bicycle. In our twenty-first century world of electronic gadgets and digital devices, the bicycle seems less thrillingly modern than quaintly mechanical. Yet its purity of purpose, efficiency of function and simplicity of design has seen it through; the bike is as useful to us now as ever. Arguably, more than ever, now that we are forced to imagine a future without limitless, cheap oil to fuel our cars and planes.

The bicycle is, in the words of the director of the Tour de France, Jean-Marie Leblanc, 'a symbol of freedom'. How true. At the macro, public policy level, a symbol of freedom from the great car economy and our oil dependency. At the personal, private level, a symbol of freedom as, for so many of us, the bicycle was a vehicle of self-discovery when we first learnt to ride one as a child and a world of possibility opened up for us. Who can live without that? However old you are, that first, dawning sense of liberation never quite leaves you. It becomes subliminal, taken for granted, only rediscovered in an explicit, realised way on those special days when the sun shines and it feels good to be alive. Every time you get on your bike and ride, that sensation is revived and experienced afresh. It's like the feeling of recognition and return you get when meeting an old friend. But always mixed with the idea of setting out, that brisk sense of hopefulness and novelty. As Jean-Marie might say, *Allez*!

Directory

United Kingdom:

Historical interest:

Historic bikes
www.hetchins.org

Wheelmen
A club for antique bike enthusiasts
www.thewheelmen.org

The Racing Bicycle
An illustrated history of the road bike.
www.theracingbicycle.com

Urban Cycling

Police registering:
www.immobilise.com

Cycle Scheme
Information about tax breaks for cyclists.
www.cyclescheme.co.uk

Cycle Training UK
Cycle Training UK is one of the largest agencies devoted to training in schools and running courses for adults.
www.ctuk.co.uk

Transport for London
Provides an excellent route planner for Londoners (follow the cycling links).
www.tfl.gov.uk

London Cycling Campaign
Aiming to make London a world-class cycling city – provides free cycle maps and very thorough information sheets.
www.lcc.org.uk

Cycle Sport

Cyclo-cross
A site dedicated to cyclo-cross coverage.
www.cyclo-cross.com

What Mountain Bike
www.whatmtb.com

Mountain Biking UK
The online wing of MBUK, the biggest selling UK-based Mountain Biking magazine.
www.mbuk.com

Road Time Trials Council (RTTC)
www.rttc.org.uk

London Cycle Sport
Contains links to local cycling groups.
www.londoncyclesport.com

Advocacy Groups and Cycling Organisations

working for cycling

The Cyclists Touring Club (CTC)
The UK's largest membership cycling organisation.
www.ctc.org.uk

JOIN THE MOVEMENT

Sustrans
The leading sustainable transport charity.
www.sustrans.org.uk

British Cycling
The governing body of cycling in the UK.
www.britishcycling.org.uk

Cycle Campaign Network CCN
The UK national federation of cycle campaign groups supporting cycling locally, regionally, nationally and in Europe.
www.cyclenetwork.org.uk

Critical Mass
www.critical-mass.org

Cycleweb
General resources and links to forums and clubs
www.cycleweb.org.uk

I'd Rather Cycle
A campaigning organisation bringing awareness to motorists, councils, pedestrians and cyclists.
www.idrathercycle.org

National Bike Week
17–25 June is the UK's annual celebration of cycling. Find out about events and rides.
www.bikeweek.org.uk

Cycling England (previously National Cycling Strategy)
A national body which coordinates the development of cycling across England.
www.nationalcyclingstrategy.org.uk

LifeCycle
Encouraging people to cycle by providing them with the skills, the knowledge and the training to get on their bikes.
www.lifecycleuk.org.uk

Why Cycle
Offers impartial advice for potential and new cyclists in the UK.
www.whycycle.co.uk

Bike-for-all
'Everything you wanted to know about cycling but were too afraid to ask.'
www.bikeforall.net

Maps and Tours

Cycle City Guides
This is a cycle map database (similar to Streetmap) that should enable you to find the cycle map for your area.
www.cyclecityguides.co.uk

Cycle-n-Sleep
A website sketching out routes for longer distance cycle rides across the UK.
www.cycle-n-sleep.co.uk

Greenways
A network of off-highway routes connecting people to the open spaces in the UK.
www.countryside.gov.uk/LAR/Recreation/Greenways

United States

National Organisations

BikeSutra
A massive cycling directory of organisations manufacturers and bike services.
www.bikesutra.com

League of American Bicyclists
Working for a bicycle-friendly America.
www.bikeleague.org

National Bike Greenway
An organisation trying to create a highway-free Greenway for cyclists that runs the length of the United States.
www.nationalbicyclegreenway.com

National Centre for Bicycling and Walking
A non-profit corporation providing consultancy, training and workshops for people who want to make their community more pedestrian and cyclist friendly.
www.bikewalk.org

Thunderhead Alliance
A coalition of 35 state and regional bicycle advocacy organisations sharing information and ideas.
www.thunderheadalliance.org

America Bikes
A coalition of eight major national bicycling organisations.
www.americabikes.org

Bikes Belong
A membership organisation with the mission to 'put people on bikes more often'.
www.bikesbelong.org

International Mountain Bicycling Association
Enhances and preserves trail opportunities for mountain bikers worldwide.
www.imba.com

Rails to Trails Conservancy
Aims to convert a nationwide network of disused rail tracks into cycle paths.
www.railstrails.org

About bicycles
Helping you choose a bike and accessories.
www.about-bicycles.com

American Bike Trails
Maps and guides to trails across the US.
www.abtrails.com

Bicycle Link
Guide to new and used bicycle prices.
www.bicyclelink.com

Bike This Way
A website that helps you find new rides in your area, and links you up with other cycle enthusiasts.
www.bikethisway.com

Cycling Reviews
Bike related news and reviews.
www.cyclingreviews.com

State Cycling Organisations

Alabama

Alabama Bicycle Coalition
www.alabike.org

Birmingham Urban Mountain Pedalers
www.bump.org

Arizona

Bicycle Inter-community Action & Salvage
www.bicas.org

Coalition of Arizona Bicyclists
www.cazbike.com

Prescott Alternative Transportation
www.prescottbikeped.org

Verde Valley Cyclists
www.vvcc.us

Arkansas

Mississippi River Trail, Inc.
www.mississippirivertrail.org

Bicycle Advocacy of Central Arkansas
www.bacar.org

California

California Bicycle Coalition
www.calbike.org

East Bay Bicycle Coalition
www.ebbc.org

Marin County Bicycle Coalition
www.marinbike.org

Peninsula Bicycle & Pedestrian Coalition
www.penbiped.org

People Power
www.peoplepower.org

Sacramento Area Bicycle Advocates
www.sacbike.org

San Diego County Bicycle Coalition
www.sdcbc.org

San Francisco Bicycle Coalition
www.sfbike.org

San Luis Obispo County Bicycle Coalition
www.slobikelane.com

**Santa Barbara
Bicycle Coaltion**
www.sbbike.org

**Silicon Valley Bicycle
Coalition**
www.svbcbikes.org

**Transportation for a
Livable City**
www.liveablecity.org

Colorado

Bicycle Colorado
www.bicyclecolo.org

**Pikes Peak Area
Bikeways Coalition**
www.trailsandopenspaces.org

Connecticut

**Connecticut Bicycle
Coalition**
www.ctbike.org

**Central Connecticut
Bicycle Alliance**
www.wecyclect.org

District of
Columbia

**Washington Area
Bicyclist Association**
www.waba.org

Florida

**Florida Bicycle
Association_**
www.floridabicycle.org/

**Safe bicycling
Coalition**
www.safebicycling.org

Georgia

**Atlanta Bicycle
Campaign**
www.atlantabike.org

Bike Roswell
www.bikeroswell.com

Georgia Bikes!
www.georgiabikes.org

Hawaii

**Hawaii Bicycling
League**
www.hbl.org

Idaho

**Teton Valley
Cycling Alliance**
www.tvtap.org

Illinois

**Chicagoland Bicycle
Federation**
www.biketraffic.org

**League of Illinois
Bicyclists**
www.bikelib.org

Wheeling Wheelmen
www.wheelmen.com

Indiana

**Indiana Bicycle
Coalition**
www.bicycleindiana.org

Iowa

Iowa Bicycle Coalition
www.iowabicyclecoalition.
org

Louisiana

**Greater New Orleans
Metro Bicycle
Coalition**
www.metrobicyclecoalition.
org

Maine

**Bicycle Coalition
of Maine**
www.BikeMaine.org

Maryland

One Less Car
www.onelesscar.org

Massachusetts

**Livable Streets
Transportation
Alliance**
www.bikethehub.org

**Massachusetts
Bicycle Coalition**
www.massbike.org

Michigan

**League of Michigan
Bicyclists**
www.lmb.org

Minnesota

**Parks & Trails Council
of Minnesota**
www.parksandtrails.org

Mississippi

**Bicycle Advocacy
Group of Mississippi**
www.bikemississippi.org

Missouri

**Missouri Bicycle
Federation**
www.mobikefed.org

**Springbike
Bicycle Club**
www.springbike.org

**St Louis Regional
Bicycle Federation**
www.slbikefed.org

Trailnet
www.trailnet.org

Montana

**Missoula Institute
for Sustainable
Transportation**
www.strans.org

Nebraska

Great Plains Bicycling Club
www.greatplainsbikeclub.org

Nevada

Silver State Bicycle Coalition
www.ssbcnv.org

New Jersey

Hoboken Bicycle Project
www.hobiken.com

New Mexico

Bicycle Coalition of New Mexico
www.bikenm.org

New York

New York Bicycling Coalition
www.nybc.net

Transportation Alternatives
www.transalt.org

Ohio

Central Ohio Bicycle Advocacy Coalition
www.cobac.org

Ohio Bicycle Federation
www.ohiobike.org

Cleveland Bikes
www.clevelandbikes.org

Oklahoma

Red Dirt Pedalers
www.reddirtpedalers.com

Oklahoma Bicycle Coalition
www.oklahomabicyclecoalition.com

Oregon

Bicycle Transportation Alliance
http://bta4bikes.org

Pennsylvania

Bicycle Access Council
www.bicycleaccess-pa.org

Bicycle Coalition of Greater Philadelphia
www.bicyclecoalition.org

Bike Pittsburgh
www.bike-pgh.org

Rhode Island

Greenways Alliance of Rhode Island
www.rigreenways.org/

Tennessee

Walk/Bike Nashville
www.walkbikenashville.org

Texas

Austin Cycling Association_Preston
www.austincycling.org

BikeHouston
www.bikehouston.org

Texas Bicycle Coalition
www.biketexas.org

Utah

Mountain Trails Foundation
www.mountaintrails.org

Vermont

Local Motion
www.localmotionvt.org

Vermont Bicycle & Pedestrian Coalition
www.vtbikeped.org

Virginia

BikeWalk
www.bikewalkvirginia.org

Bicycling Alliance
www.vabike.org

Washington

Bicycle Alliance of Washington
www.bicyclealliance.org

Cascade Bicycle Club Advocacy Committee
www.cascade.org/home

West Virginia

Mountain State Wheelers Bicycle Club
www.mountainstatewheelers.org

Wisconsin

Bicycle Federation of Wisconsin
www.bfw.org

Wyoming

Friends of Pathways
www.jhpathways.com

Canada

British Columbia Cycling Coalition
www.bccc.bc.ca

**Greater Victoria
Cycling Coalition**
Darren
www.gvcc.bc.ca

Australia

**Bicycle Federation
of Australia**
A non profit organisation
promoting healthy
activity for Australians.
www.bfa.asn.au

**Australian
Bicycle Council**
www.abc.dotars.gov.au

more people cycling more often

Bicycle Victoria
News and links to local
and national websites.
www.bv.com.au

Bicycles.net
A majpr web portal
for Australian cyclists
with links to all the key
organisations.
www.bicycles.net.au

Europe

**European Cyclists
Federation**
Promoting cycling and
cycle-friendly policies
throughout Europe.
www.ecf.com

Tour de France
The official website of
the Tour.
www.letour.fr

**Bicycle Policy Audit
(BYPAD)**
www.bypad.org

Manufacturers:

Marin
www.marinbikes.com

Specialized
www.specialized.com

Ridgeback
www.ridgebackbikes.
co.uk

Trek
www.trekbikes.com

cannondale *feel it*

Cannondale
www.cannondale.com

FUJI
Bicycles Since 1899
SIMPLY BETTER.

Fuji Bikes
Leading manufacturer of
track bikes.
www.fujibikes.com

Giant Bicycles
www.giant-bicycles.com

Raleigh
www.raleighbikes.com

Pashley
For all your cycle-trailer
needs.
www.pashley.co.uk

Dawes
www.dawescycles.com

Raleigh
www.raleighbikes.com

Velowalker
Lovely wooden kids bikes.
www.velowalker.com

Islabikes
High quality
childrens' bikes.
www.islabikes.co.uk

BROMPTON

Brompton
The famous folding bikes.
www.bromptonbicycle.co.uk

Rapha.

Rapha
Classy, up-market cycle
clothing and accessories.
www.rapha.cc

Shimano
www.shimano-europe.com

Respro
Pollution masks and
other accessories for
urban cycling.
www.respro.com

Zyro
High performance
accessories.
www.zyro.co.uk

Selected Bibliography

Baker, Arnie, *Smart Cycling: Successful Training and Racing for Riders of All Levels*, New York: Fireside/Simon & Schuster, 1997.

Ballantine, Richard, *Richard's 21st Century Bicycle Book*, London: Pan, 2000.

Bell, Trudie, The Essential Bicycle Commuter, New York: McGraw-Hill, 1998.

Edwards, Sally and Sally Reed, T*he Heart Rate Monitor Book for Cyclists*, Boulder, CO: Velo Press, Boulder, 2002.

Fotheringham, William, *A Century of Cycling: The Classic Races and Legendary Champions*, London: Mitchell Beazley, 2003.

Fotheringham, William, *Put Me Back on My Bike: In Search of Tom Simpson*, London: Yellow Jersey Press, 2003.

Friel, Joe, *The Cyclist's Training Bible*, London: A&C Black, 2003.

Herlihy, David, *Bicycle: The History*, London: Yale University Press, 2004.

Hilton, Tim, *One More Kilometre and We're in the Showers*, London: HarperCollins, 2004.

Imhoff, Dan, *Fat Tire*, San Francsisco: Chronicle Books, 1996.

Kimmage, Paul, *A Rough Ride*, London: Yellow Jersey Press, 2001.

McGum, James, *On Your Bicycle*, London: John Murray, 1987.

Milson, Fred, *The Bike Book*, Yeovil Somerset: Haynes Publishing, 2004.

Moore, Tim, *French Revolutions: Cycling the Tour de France*, London: Vintage, 2002.

The Official Tour de France Centennial 1903–2003, London: Weidenfeld & Nicolson, 2003.

Pavelka, Ed, *Bicycling Magazine's Complete Book of Road Cycling Skills: Your Guide to Riding Faster, Stronger, Longer, and Safer*, Pennsylvania: Rodale Press, Emmaus, 1998.

Penn, Rob, *Bicycling Along the World's Most Exceptional Routes*, London: Abbe Mille Press, 2005.

Perry, David, *Bike Cult: The Ultimate Guide to Human-Powered Vehicles*, New York: Four Walls Eight Windows, 1995.

Sidwells, Chris, *The Complete Bike Book*, Chris Sidwells, London: Dorling Kindersley, 2003.

Picture Credits

2   From the personal collection of Oscar Cassander www.home.wanadoo.nl/peugotshow

3   From the personal collection of Sheldon Brown. www.sheldonbrown.org

4   Library of Congress, reproduction number: LC-UZC4-6645

5   From the Dayton C. Miller photograph collection, given to the Library of Congress

6   From the personal collection of Oscar Cassander From the personal collection of Sheldon Brown

7   From www.critical-mass.org

10 Courtesy of Rydor Bike Shop, Austin Minnesota

11 Fred Hultstrand History in Pictures Collection, at the Librar y of Congress, NDIRS NDSU, Fargo

11 Courtesy of www. theracingbicycle.com

12 Courtesy of Rydor Bike Shop

13 From the Advertising Ephemera Collection, Library of Congress, reproduction number: A0054

15 Library of Congress reproduction number: LC-USZC40-12098

16 Courtesy of the Solomon Guggenheim Collection

18 Library of Congress, Advertising Ephemera Collection, reproduction number: A0053

19 Library of Congress, Robert Runyon Collection, reproduction number: 08637

21 Library of Congress, reproduction number: LC-USF34-065228-D-DLC From the personal collection of Mick Knapton

22 Courtesy of Cannondale

23 Courtesy of Tom Lynch

24 Courtesy of Flash at www. hetchins.org

25 Courtesy of Specialized

26 Photography by Metin Alsanjak

27 www.criticalmass.org

31 Courtesy of Stephen Carter, Wheelman

36 Courtesy of Paul van Roekel and Anja Graf

37 Photography by Sion Parkinson

43 Courtesy of Cannondale

47 Courtesy of Marin, Cannondale, Specialized and Giant

50 Courtesy of Specialized

50 Courtesy of Giant

52 Courtesy of Fuji

54 Courtesy of Specialized

55 Courtesy of Tom Lynch

56 Courtesy of Cannondale

57 Courtesy of Brompton

60 Courtesy of Abus and Kryptonite

62 Courtesy of Zyro

66 Courtesy of Specialized and Zyro

69 Courtesy of Abus

71 Library of Congress, Fred Hulstrand History in Pictures Collection

86 Courtesy of pedbike

88 Courtesy of pedbike

89 Photography by Sion Parkinson

90 Photography by Metin Alsanjak

94 Courtesy of Rapha

97 Courtesy of Respro

101 Courtesy of National Cycling Strategy

103 Photography by Sion Parkinson

104 Courtesy of Fat Tire beer

108 Courtesy of Steve Taylor at Transport for London

110 Courtesy of Cycle Training: www. cycletraining.co.uk

118 Photography by Sion Parkinson

121 Photography by Alistair Humphries

126 Courtesy of Tom Lynch

127 Courtesy of Tom Lynch

129 Courtesy of Christian Frommert at T-Mobile.

130 Courtesy of Christian Frommert at T-Mobile.

134 Courtesy of Jay Van de Velde at: www.theracingbicycle.com Courtesy of Christian Frommert at T-mobile.

135 Courtesy of Jay Van de Velde at: www.theracingbicycle.com

136 Courtesy of David Abrutat

138 www.theracingbicycle.com

139 Courtesy of Christian Frommert at T-Mobile.

141 From the private collection of Sheldon Brown.

142 Courtesy of Christian Frommert at T-Mobile.

144 Courtesy of Christian Frommert at T-Mobile.

146 Courtesy of Jay Van de Velde at: www.theracingbicycle.com

147 Courtesy of Christian Frommert at T-Mobile.

153 Courtesy of Jay Van de Velde at: www.theracingbicycle.com

159 Courtesy of Tom Lynch.

166 Courtesy of Paul van Roekel and Anja de Graaf www.cyclingaroundtheworld.nl

168 www.critical-mass.org

169 Courtesy of National Cycling Strategy

170 From www.EcolQ.com

171 Courtesy of Bjarne Greg Jensen at Aarhus Bycykel

173 Courtesy of Lorraine Gamman at the DAC centre

175 Courtesy of Garmin UK

176 Courtesy of Eric Stokker at Shimano Europe

177 Courtesy of Tony at www.raleigh-chopper.com

179 Courtesy of Paul van Roekel and Anja de Graaf www.cyclingaroundtheworld.nl

Thanks

All the manufacturers, bicycle clubs and enthusiasts who were so generous with their information, imagery and experiences.

Rosalind Knight for her hard graft and help on research.

Draught Associates
Amy Sackville
Holly Pester

Dean Taylor
Sheldon Brown
Oscar Casander
David Abrutat
Christian Frommert
Vaughn Trevisanut
Paul Van Roekel and Anja de Graaf
Mike Tischer at the Rydjor Bike Shop
Jay Van de Velde at theracingbicycle.com
Alistair Humphries
Metin Alsanjak
Sion Parkinson
All of whom helped illustrate this book

Steve Taylor at TFL

Tom Lynch, Lucy and Wendy Garner, Raoul Morley
Dan Simon, Stephen Carter, Nick Harvey
Helen Cooney and Andy Dyson– for their time and insights.

146 Courtesy of Jay Van de Velde at:

Black Dog Publishing

Architecture Art Design Fashion History
Photography Theory and Things

theguardian

This book is published in association with Guardian Books. Guardian
Books is an imprint of Guardian Newspapers Limited. The Guardian
is a registered trademark of Guardian Media Group plc.

Text by Matt Seaton
Edited by Cigalle Hanaor
Design by Paul Stafford at Draught Associates

Black Dog Publishing Limited
Unit 4.4 Tea Building
56 Shoreditch High Street
London
E1 6JJ

Tel: +44 (0)20 7613 1922
Fax: +44 (0)20 7613 1944
Email: info@bdp.demon.co.uk

www.bdpworld.com

British Library Cataloguing-in-Publication Data.

A CIP record for this book is available from the British Library.

ISBN 1 904772 40 4